C C
MC
PACK GUIDE
S0-AWW-254

THE BEST
Rocky
Mountain
National Park
HIKES

THE SHINING MOUNTAINS GROUP
of
THE COLORADO MOUNTAIN CLUB
with
WARD LUTHI

The Colorado Mountain Club Press
Golden, Colorado

The Best Rocky Mountain National Park Hikes
© 2013 by The Colorado Mountain Club

PUBLISHED BY

The Colorado Mountain Club Press
710 Tenth Street, Suite 200, Golden, Colorado 80401
303-996-2743   e-mail: cmcpress@cmc.org

Founded in 1912, The Colorado Mountain Club is the largest outdoor recreation, education, and conservation organization in the Rocky Mountains. Look for our books at your local bookstore or outdoor retailer or online at www.cmc.org/store.

Erika K. Arroyo: design, composition, and production
Eduard B. Avis: copy editor
John Gascoyne: series editor
Ward Luthi: project manager
Christian Green: publisher

CONTACTING THE PUBLISHER
We would appreciate it if readers would alert us to any errors or outdated information by contacting us at the address above.

DISTRIBUTED TO THE BOOK TRADE BY
The Mountaineers Books, 1001 SW Klickitat Way, Suite 201, Seattle, WA 98134, 800-553-4453, www.mountaineersbooks.org

TOPOGRAPHIC MAPS are copyright 2009 and were created using National Geographic TOPO! Outdoor Recreation software (www.natgeomaps.com; 800-962-1643).

COVER PHOTO: Keyboard of the Winds and Pagoda Mountain, as seen from Glacier Creek.
Photo by Frank Burzynski

We gratefully acknowledge the financial support of the people of Colorado through the Scientific and Cultural Facilities District of greater Denver for our publishing activities.

WARNING: Although there has been an effort to make the trail descriptions in this book as accurate as possible, some discrepancies may exist between the text and the trails in the field. Hiking in mountainous areas—and canyons and deserts as well—is a high-risk activity. This guidebook is not a substitute for your experience and common sense. The users of this guidebook assume full responsibility for their own safety. Weather, terrain conditions, and individual abilities must be considered before undertaking any of the hikes in this guide.

First Edition

ISBN 978-1-937052-05-8

Printed in Korea

TO ROCKY MOUNTAIN
NATIONAL PARK

Almost invariably, dedications are directed toward people, folks whose contributions to an enterprise, a group, or a place warrant special praise. We've tried to acknowledge such people elsewhere in this book. This dedication is to a place.

We invite you to join us in honoring Rocky Mountain National Park. The Park and its extraordinary components—flora and fauna, streams and lakes, trees and mountains—comprise one of America's favorite national preserves.

Stand beside a group of first-timers to the Park. You can almost see their jaws drop, and then drop again. Spend time with veteran hikers, climbers, and other serious Park enthusiasts—their appreciation is intense, it seldom diminishes. It is difficult to enjoy the Park without experiencing this contagious sense of awe.

Rocky Mountain National Park is many things; it is not, however, a theme park where all elements are tightly controlled and all outcomes are guaranteed. The observation that "the mountain doesn't care" is as true today as when it was first coined many years ago.

As you enjoy and appreciate Rocky Mountain National Park, we encourage you to consider some present-day realities. Some of our recommended hikes will have you viewing land scorched by the 2012 fire. We encourage you to explore these areas as well as the undamaged ones. Examine your own assumptions and consider what you have learned about the origins of such fires, and also about diminished snow packs in the high country. If you determine that humans are part of the problem, consider that they also must have a role in the solutions.

There are common sense practices that will help protect the park, its denizens, and its physical beauty—such as staying on the designated trail and avoiding short-cutting on switchbacks

Marmot posing for the camera.

PHOTO BY MARLENE BORNEMAN

Gray jay on Lulu City Trail.

or letting wild animals stay wild by not feeding them and observing them only from a respectful distance.

A present-day reality is that the Park relies in part on private citizen funding for many objectives—acquisition of new land, maintenance of trails, and a host of other needs. If you can help, go to the Rocky Mountain Nature Association website and see which program you'd like to support.

It is with deep appreciation and high regard that the Colorado Mountain Club dedicates this book to Rocky Mountain National Park.

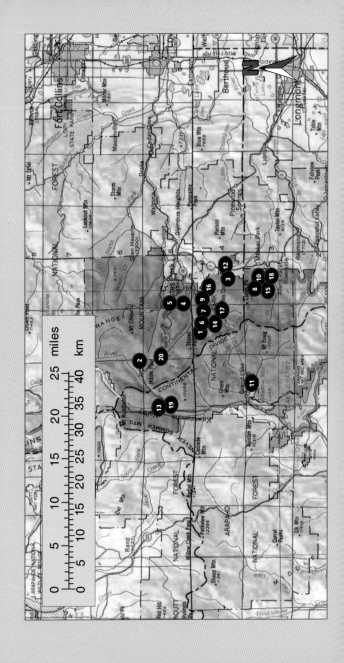

CONTENTS

A beaver's reflection.

FOREWORD

In 2007, the Colorado Mountain Club began an ambitious project—the publication of "pack guides" for those parts of the state most enjoyed by CMC members and other hikers. The guides are small enough to slip into a pocket or day pack, large enough to contain most of the information that hikers need for an enjoyable and safe adventure. Each guidebook features the 20 hikes selected by members of the local CMC group as their own favorites. (*The Best Denver Hikes*, with Bob Dawson as project manager, covers a wider hiking area than most and contains 30 hikes.) Each guide includes hikes with a range of difficulty, some handicapped accessible trails, and some kid-friendly ones.

The pack guides, conceived by Alan "Bear" Stark, former CMC publisher, and designed by his colleague Alan Bernhard, were intended to have high eye-appeal, with attractive full-color photos and maps. The guides contain pertinent data, with degree of difficulty, round-trip distance and time, elevation achieved, nearest landmark, and applicable maps included for each trail. The "Comment" section for each trail discusses special features of that trail and the surrounding area; the "Route" portion provides sufficient details to allow hikers to arrive safely at, and return from, the hike's destination; and the "Getting There" section instructs the reader about how to drive to the trailhead.

CMC's pack guides have an effective production structure. After CMC groups have determined the hikes to be included in their book, one member is asked to be the author for each trail. Each author is responsible for hiking the trail, writing a coherent description of it, photographing unique aspects, and submitting a map of his or her hike. This work is compiled and edited by the project manager for that book. The series editor works with the project manager to bring the book to completion.

For many folks, their work with one pack guide has led to involvement with others. Jeff Eisele, who did a trail report for *The Best Fort Collins Hikes*, went on to become the project manager for *The Best Durango Hikes,* and then became the editor for an in-progress pack guide for the Telluride area. Rod Martinez, project manager for *The Best Grand Junction Hikes*, later was the project manager for the Telluride book. Joe and Frédérique Grim, trail writers for the Fort Collins book, authored *Comanche Peaks Wilderness Area: Hiking and Snowshoeing Guide*. Greg Long, project manager for *The Best Colorado Springs Hikes*, is the author of *The Best Southern Front Range Hikes*.

Three new pack guides were published in 2013, including *The Best Vail Valley Hikes*, with Nathan Free as project manager, and *The Best Estes Park Hikes,* for which Ward Luthi was project manager.

The book that you are holding, *The Best Rocky Mountain National Park Hikes,* is the latest addition to the series. It has at least two ambitions: to make you stop whatever else you may be doing and lace up your boots, and to instill in you, as in all of us, a sense of awe and a desire to protect the amazing natural heritage that is Rocky Mountain National Park.

—John Gascoyne
Series Editor,
CMC Pack Guides

ACKNOWLEDGMENTS

Pioneers, adventurous souls, explorers, committed conservationists, talented writers, and great photographers—all terms I use to describe the authors for this pack guide for Rocky Mountain National Park.

In their spare moments, these wild-at-heart souls strike out to explore Rocky Mountain National Park, eyes alert for special views, hidden corners, great lunch spots, or perfect places to view wildlife. As they move along each path, they weigh the number of ups and downs, roughness of terrain, and time required in order to decide whether a trail is easy, moderate, or more difficult. Then they capture what they feel is the essence of the trail, or a view that illustrates the special beauty of a particular area, and write it all up so we have a trail map for our own adventures.

Join me in saluting the creative talents and passionate dedication of the following individuals in guiding us along truly beautiful paths into the heart of Rocky Mountain National Park, the jewel of our natural heritage in Colorado.

Jack Powers   Kurt Worrell
Amy Crow   Rudy Schmiedt
Danielle Raker Poole   Sallie Varner
Gordon Shaw Novak Jr.   Alan Apt
Caroline Blackwell Schmiedt   Christian Green

Once again, I want to express heartfelt appreciation to the Shining Mountains Group of the Colorado Mountain Club. This cadre of individuals, which includes authors of this guide, is committed to the protection and preservation of Rocky Mountain National Park and to helping everyone learn to travel safely and enjoyably in the Colorado outdoors. Each year CMC offers more than 600 outings into the Park.

Having had the privilege to work for the National Park Service as a staff member for the President's Commission on

Americans Outdoors, I have great admiration for the men and women who work every day to ensure the integrity, beauty, and health of Rocky Mountain National Park. Running a park as large and heavily visited as Rocky requires the best, and I know that's exactly who we have here in our Park. Many, many thanks to each and every one of you.

A special thanks to Christian Green, our publisher and author of the Cub Lake Trail description in this guide. Christian's work at the helm of the Colorado Mountain Club publications has been exemplary, and his support and encouragement have been instrumental in getting this guide published.

And, of course, a big heartfelt thanks goes to my editor and good friend, John Gascoyne. This is the second time John has graciously asked me to serve as project manager for a pack guide, the first being the Estes Park guide. We've hiked many trails together, debated how best to present the trail descriptions submitted by our talented authors, and dreamed about where we would head for our next adventures.

To you, our readers, my enduring gratitude—first, for using our guides to chart your adventures, and second, for your lifelong love and support of our National Parks.

I look forward to seeing you on the trails . . .

—Ward Luthi,
Project Manager

Introduction

Welcome to the majestic world of Rocky Mountain National Park. If you're a frequent visitor, you have a good idea of why this locale is such a popular destination for adventurers from around the globe. There is so much to see, appreciate, and learn from in the Park that even the most experienced hikers keep coming back.

If you're new to the Park, you may feel a bit overwhelmed by the wealth of available hiking and recreation options. No worries—this pack guide will help you make some righteous choices.

> **Caveat—on maps and map scales**
>
> In producing this pack guide, we have endeavored to provide the most accurate information possible. This striving for accuracy includes the map segments which follow each trail description. Many of the trails indicated by the red lines, however, include contours, ups and downs, and switchbacks that cannot be depicted on a small map. Thus, with some maps, you may find what looks like a variance between the stated length of the trail and the length of the trail when compared to the scale indicator.
>
> For every trail described in this guide, we list relevant, larger-scale maps of the area you will be hiking in—such as Trails Illustrated and USGS maps. It is always a good practice to secure these larger maps, study them, and understand where the smaller map from the guide fits within the larger map. The best practice is to carry both maps on your hike.

The Best Rocky Mountain National Park Hikes can be looked at as something of a "how-to" book. Although there are a great many hiking trails in the park, and other useful hiking guides also in print, this pack guide contains a wealth of information compiled by a number of experienced and capable hikers on what we believe are truly some of the best trails you can find. Let these experienced folks show you the way.

Some suggestions in using this guide to best advantage:

- First, just scan the book and enjoy the great photographs. On a second pass, try to decide which kinds of hikes will likely work best for you—such as easier ones for families, trailblazers with disabilities, and

At the Cub Lake trailhead.

PHOTO BY CHRISTIAN GREEN

people acclimating to the high elevations in the park. Check out the moderate to more difficult options if those fit your preferences and capabilities.

- In narrowing your choices, consider other variables—such as how far away one trailhead is compared to another and how long it would take you to get to each. Engage in some up-to-the-moment information gathering—if you know when sunrise will occur, you can begin hiking at daybreak; if you know that the weather will be challenging on a given day, you may choose to stay indoors with that book you've been wanting to read.

- When you do select a trail, study all of the information that we've provided about it; carefully study your hike before taking that first step.

Become familiar with other content in your pack guide. Learn and observe all of the elements of the Ten Essentials. More helpful information is available at www.cmc.org.

We wish you great adventures in Rocky Mountain National Park, truly one of Colorado's most precious crown jewels.

In adventure,
Ward Luthi

The Ten Essentials Systems

This pack guide is published by the Colorado Mountain Club—now in its 101st year of fostering safe practices and environmental stewardship in the wild areas of our state. Every hiker—experienced or beginner—will benefit by studying these principles, practicing them, and teaching them to others.

1. **Hydration.** Each day-hiker should carry a minimum of two quarts, or liters, of water. In more arid regions, carry more. A good practice is to have lots of extra water in your vehicle—drink a good deal of it before setting out and save some for the end of your adventure. Consider purchasing a Camelbak® or similar soft carrier that fits inside of, or attached to, your daypack—having a drinking tube close to your face while you are hiking is a proven way to stay hydrated. Whatever you do, continue drinking while you are on the trail—if you wait until you are thirsty, you've likely waited too long.

2. **Nutrition.** Don't skimp on ingesting energy-producing foods. Eat a large and healthy breakfast before hiking. Pack a good lunch with lots of fruits, vegetables, and carbohydrates. Carry quick energy snacks such as trail mix and nutrition bars—as much as anything, good nutrition will help keep your mind clear for decision making.

3. **Sun protection.** Apply—and re-apply—sunscreen with at least a 45 SPF rating; use lip balm. Wear sunglasses and a wide-brimmed hat. Keep in mind that the sun's UV rays at 10,000 feet are roughly 25 percent stronger than at sea level. Also, keep in mind that snow reflects as much as 90 percent of the sunshine, so it strikes you a second time.

4. **Insulation.** Carry extra clothing to fit different critical needs. Colorado's weather can change in very short intervals and you want to be prepared to cope with Nature's surprises. More than anything, you want to stay warm and dry—so pack accordingly. Cotton is the real enemy here, leave it home; wool and synthetic materials will serve you well. Layering is a critical component, especially in cold or wet weather; put things on or take them off as the situation changes. Hypothermia, a potential life-threatening decrease in body temperature, is something that should be taken seriously. Carry a warm hat, warm gloves, and an extra pair of socks. Be prepared for wet weather with a parka, or shell, and rain pants. Experienced hikers spend the little extra time needed to make clothing changes as often as their situation requires.

5. **Navigation.** Basic route-finding abilities are a critical skill for all hikers, even on what seem to be clearly marked trails. Learn minimal proficiency with a map and compass. Before you hike, use a larger map of the entire area and study your route. A global positioning system (GPS) unit can add to your capabilities.

6. **Illumination.** A flashlight, with extra batteries, is an essential part of your gear. A better idea is to carry a headlamp, which allows both hands to be free. Nighttime hiking can be hazardous—avoid it except in emergencies. A second light source is recommended.

7. **First Aid.** There are good hiker's first-aid kits available or you can create one that best fits your needs and preferences. Consider including:

   - A bandana—which has many uses, including as an arm sling or emergency tourniquet
   - Duct tape—can go over a blister or wound, provide emergency repairs, and serve many other uses

Bear in bathtub.

- Hygiene supplies—liquid soap, latex gloves, toilet paper, and Ziploc bags—nothing is left in the woods
- A chart or booklet on how to deal with medical emergencies

8. **Fire.** Open fires in the woods should be considered dangerous and avoided when at all possible. If emergency circumstances force you to build an open fire—for warmth or cooking—use all possible care. You do want to carry fire ribbon or waterproof matches in a watertight container. Hardened tree sap and dry pine needles can help get a fire going. If you will be cooking on the trail, use a hiker's portable stove and fuel stored in a very tight metal container.

9. **Repair kit and emergency tools.** Carry a small pocket knife or, better, a multi-use tool that has a decent blade. Duct tape and electrician's tape can

serve many uses. Carry a signal mirror and whistle in your tool kit.

10. **Emergency shelter.** Carry some nylon cord and a space blanket or a bivouac sack. A large plastic leaf bag can have multiple uses—temporary rainwear, a cover for your pack, or a survival shelter. Use the bag on your way out to carry trash left behind by less thoughtful hikers.

OTHER USEFUL SAFETY MEASURES

Tell someone where you'll be hiking and when you plan to return.

Leave a note on your dashboard, readable from outside your vehicle, that provides information about your hike—where you are heading, when you will return, how many are in your party, and contact information for family or friends.

Carry a SPOT—this satellite-activated personal locator can tell emergency personnel that you need help and where to find you. These devices' retail cost is around $100 or more, but they can save lives. When you're not hiking, keep the device in your vehicle for emergency use.

A NOTE ON HYPOTHERMIA

This is the phenomenon where wetness or cold, or a combination of the two, chills the body and results in a lowering of its core temperature. When not addressed, hypothermia can be fatal. Water is the severest conductor of heat, and more cases of hypothermia have been recorded in summer than in winter. Cotton should be considered dangerous—it retains water and chills you down. Wool and synthetics tend to wick the water away and can retain heat even when damp. Gear up at the first sign of rain; change out of wet clothes at the first opportunity.

LEAVE NO TRACE

We owe it to present and future generations to care for the wild places: if you pack it in, pack it out—leave only footprints:

- Plan ahead and prepare for the cleanest possible adventure.
- Stay on the trail and don't shortcut on switchbacks; camp on durable surfaces—such as rock or sand. Above timberline, hike on rocks and avoid damaging the tundra. When more than one person is off trail, spread out so you don't start destructive new "social" trails.
- Dispose of all waste properly—including that deposited by your dog. Pack it in, pack it out.
- Leave what you find—look at it, take a photo; leave it for the next person.
- Minimize campfire impacts—think small, keep the fuel within the fire circle; unless it is a permanent fire pit, destroy all traces of your fire before leaving your campsite. Forest fires have started from small campfires or their smoldering embers; be extremely cautious in this regard—the best practice is to soak down your fire site.
- Respect wildlife—don't feed them anything; don't intrude on their feeding and breeding areas. Moose deserve your complete respect—they are considered by experts to be the most dangerous creatures in the Colorado woods.
- Be considerate of animals and other humans in the woods—don't play radios or create other unnecessary noise. Part of the lure of the woods is the healing sound of wind through the trees and the murmur of a stream.

Let's Talk Weather

(Especially if you're new to Colorado)

There's a raggedy old saying that if you don't like the weather in Colorado, just wait five minutes and it's sure to change.

Okay, that's a bit preposterous, but it does carry a kernel of truth—Colorado weather conditions can change fairly suddenly and fairly radically. You may start out on your hike in bright sunshine at 9 a.m. and run into rain, possibly with lightning, a few hours along the trail.

No, you can't change the weather, but you can employ a number of strategies for coping with it:

- *Go online and look for local weather reporting sources.* Then, determine short-term weather trends by examining what has happened in prior days and what the predictions are for the day of your hike and for a few days afterward.

- *Forget the 9 a.m., lazy-bones departure.* In the Colorado high country, weather changes often occur in the early to later afternoon. We don't advocate hiking in the dark, but being at the trailhead as the sun is peeking up in the east can often add a few hours of clear weather to your adventure.

- *Be willing to turn back.* That summit you want to bag will still be there tomorrow and the next day. If your sky watching reveals large thunderheads and you can hear rumbling thunder in the direction you're heading, you're better off turning around. If you find an experienced Colorado hiker who claims to have never turned back, you are dealing with a big fibber. When I

Flattop—looking toward Mills Lake.   PHOTO BY WARD LUTHI

feel the need to hightail it back to the low country, I'll make an X in the trail with my hiking pole and pretend that it marks the exact end of where I wanted to go in the first place. A mind game, yes, but it helps the ego.

- *Dress for weather success.* Elsewhere in this guidebook, we talk about equipment and items of clothing that can keep you warm and dry on the trail. You can still pack light and carry the essentials.

1. Bear Lake Trail

BY JACK POWERS

MAPS	Trails Illustrated, Rocky Mountain National Park, Number 200 USGS, McHenrys Peak Quadrangle 7.5 minute
ELEVATION GAIN	20 feet
RATING	Easy
ROUND-TRIP DISTANCE	0.5 miles
ROUND-TRIP TIME	20 minutes
NEAREST LANDMARK	Estes Park

COMMENT: Bear Lake is one of the most popular sites in Rocky Mountain National Park. The large parking lot by the lake attests to both its popularity and the fact that the lake is a jumping off spot for many other popular hikes. Trails leading from the lake or the parking lot connect to popular destinations in all directions.

This is not to say that Bear Lake is without its own merits. Hallett Peak dominates the view to the west, creating a classic combination of water and mountain. This panorama is usually the first view the visitor experiences and it leaves a lasting impression. Longs Peak and the Keyboard of the Winds can be seen farther along the trail. This vista inspired the artwork on the reverse side of the Colorado quarter-dollar coin. A large aspen grove on the north side of the lake adds spectacular color in the fall.

Bear Lake can be reached on many winter days and can be the starting point for snowshoeing around the lake or going to other nearby destinations.

Bear Lake Trail is partially handicapped accessible. Be aware, however, there are multiple spots with inclines greater than 8 percent, including some as great as 16 percent. There is also a set of log "steps" on the southwest side

Fall colors around Bear Lake.

of the lake. Although these inclines are short in length, they can be formidable barriers for a wheelchair and assistance may be required. There is an excellent sign near the entrance depicting the grades around the lake. The sign is reproduced in the "Access Rocky" brochure, which can be downloaded from the Park website.

The loop around the lake also serves as an interpretive nature trail, with 30 stops. A brochure describing the trail can be purchased at the information window at the upper end of the parking lot. Topics covered include geology, weather, flora, fauna, and Park history.

GETTING THERE: Bear Lake is a little over 9 miles from the Beaver Meadows entrance on US 36. Proceed about 300 yards past the entrance tollbooths, and turn left onto Bear Lake Road. Continue on this road until it terminates at the large Bear Lake Parking Lot.

Bear Lake is also a stop on the park's free bus system. Check at the Visitors Center for bus information, because the routes are subject to change.

THE ROUTE: The lake is about 200 feet from the upper end of the parking lot. Park rangers and volunteers are usually available at this point to provide information.

Hallett Peak reflected in Bear Lake.   PHOTO BY JACK POWERS

Circling the lake in a counterclockwise direction (a right turn) will take the hiker to the first scenic overlook. There is an excellent view of the lake and Hallett Peak at this point. Early morning visitors may find the waters calm enough to serve as a mirror, with Hallett Peak and the trees on the opposite shore reflected on the lake surface.

A short distance farther along the trail a kiosk marks the start of a trail to numerous Park destinations: Flattop Mountain, the Fern-Odessa Gorge, and Bierstadt Lake, among others.

A short distance past the kiosk, Longs Peak, the Keyboard of the Winds, and Pagoda Mountain come into view. The resemblance to the Colorado quarter is unmistakable.

Continuing to the south side of the lake, you encounter more short inclines and more shade. There is one last overlook on the south side, not too far from the entrance. This is a great spot to see and photograph the fall colors on the opposite shore. It is also a favorite spot in all seasons for visitors to pose for their "been there" pictures. Return to the parking lot by the same short trail.

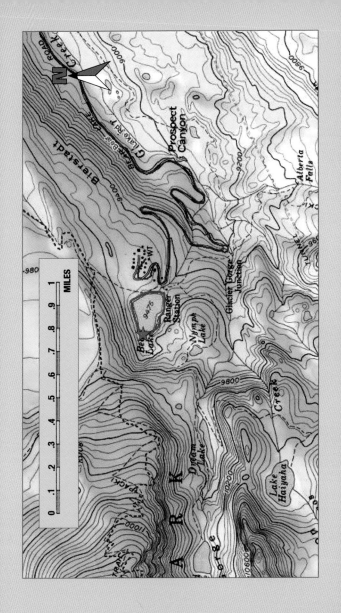

2. Chapin, Chiquita, and Ypsilon Mountains

BY CAROLINE BLACKWELL SCHMIEDT

MAPS	Trails Illustrated, Rocky Mountain National Park, Number 200 USGS, Trail Ridge Quadrangle 7.5 Minute
ELEVATION GAIN	3,200 feet
RATING	Difficult
ROUND-TRIP DISTANCE	9 miles
ROUND-TRIP TIME	7 hours
NEAREST LANDMARK	Estes Park

COMMENT: On a Saturday afternoon in August 1999, I was hunkered down in the saddle between Mount Chapin and Mount Chiquita, taking cover from an intense thunderstorm that was producing high winds and hail. I was lucky that day, but gained respect for just how quickly thunderstorms can develop in the high mountains. With a trailhead elevation of 11,000 feet, most of the hike to Chapin, Chiquita, and Ypsilon mountains is above timberline. Consequently, the best time of year to hike to these summits is in September when summer afternoon thunderstorms give way to clear fall days. Whenever you do go, be sure to watch the weather forecast carefully. There is little shelter to be found once you have begun hiking in this area. A very early morning start on a clear day will be required to reach all three summits safely. Don't worry if you don't make it to all three in one day; each summit is a great destination by itself.

Chapin, Chiquita, and Ypsilon mountains are prominent peaks located within the Mummy Range. Towering over Horseshoe Park, Chiquita and Ypsilon rise to over 13,000 feet, while Chapin reaches an elevation of 12,454 feet. Each of these

Chapin, Chiquita, and Ypsilon.   PHOTO BY CAROLINE BLACKWELL SCHMIEDT

peaks is characterized by broad northwest-facing slopes and jagged, southeast-facing cliffs. Old Fall River Road provides access to these summits, via the Chapin Pass Trailhead.

GETTING THERE: From the junction of US 34 and 36 in Estes Park, continue west on US 34 5.0 miles to the Fall River entrance to Rocky Mountain National Park. Enter the Park and continue another 2.0 miles to Endovalley Road. Turn right and follow this road for 2.0 miles to the start of Old Fall River Road. This is a one-way gravel road with many exposed hairpin turns and is closed in winter. Follow Old Fall River Road for 7.0 miles to the Chapin Pass trailhead on your right. Parking is limited, but there are a few areas on the left side where you can pull off the road safely. After your hike, continue on Old Fall River Road another 2.0 miles to the Alpine Visitor Center and the junction with Hwy 34. Turn left on Hwy 34 to return to Estes Park.

THE ROUTE: Stop at the trailhead and take a look at the Chapin Pass kiosk. The trail begins to the right of this kiosk and climbs steadily for the first 0.1 mile to a trail junction. Turn right at this junction and follow the sign indicating the Chapin, Chiquita, and Ypsilon summits. From here, the trail continues through a forest and descends slightly before crossing a log bridge. After leaving the bridge, the trail climbs steeply up a series of stone steps. Continue on to another trail junction. Veer right at this junction, following the unimproved trail to the summits.

The unimproved trail ascends above timberline and contours eastward along the north flank of Mount Chapin. Follow this trail about 1.0 mile from the junction to reach the pass between Mount Chapin and Mount Chiquita. To climb Mount Chapin, stop about 0.1 mile before reaching the pass. Turn southeast and climb off trail steeply across the tundra 0.5 mile, gaining 400 feet in elevation to the summit. A stone windbreak marks the summit and is a great place to enjoy the spectacular views of Horseshoe Park below. To reach the other summits, return to the trail and continue to the pass between Mount Chapin and Mount Chiquita. This is a good time to evaluate the weather conditions before proceeding farther.

From the pass, the unimproved trail climbs steeply northeast to the summit of Mount Chiquita, gaining 1,000 feet of elevation. Here the trail becomes more difficult to follow but is marked by cairns. A stone windbreak at the summit of Mount Chiquita provides a nice spot to rest and enjoy the wonderful views, including an impressive view of Mount Ypsilon to the north.

From the summit of Mount Chiquita, descend 300 feet northwest to the saddle between Mount Chiquita and Mount Ypsilon. From the saddle, follow the faint trail and cairns up the broad southwest flank of Mount Ypsilon, gaining 700 feet in elevation to the summit. A stone windbreak marks the summit. Wonderful views of the Spectacle Lakes can be seen from the south edge of the summit area, along with views of the seldom-visited Desolation Peaks to the northwest.

Return to the saddle between Mount Ypsilon and Mount Chiquita. Then, contour southward along the northwest flank of Mount Chiquita to rejoin the trail. Descend to the pass between Mount Chiquita and Mount Chapin. Return to the trailhead by retracing the route described.

3. Chasm Lake

BY GORDON S. NOVAK JR.

MAPS	Trails Illustrated, Rocky Mountain National Park, Number 200, or Longs and McHenrys Peak, Number 301 USGS, Longs Peak Quadrangle 7.5 minute
ELEVATION GAIN	2,380 feet
RATING	Moderate–difficult
ROUND-TRIP DISTANCE	8.4 miles
ROUND-TRIP TIME	6 hours
NEAREST LANDMARK	Estes Park

COMMENT: Chasm Lake is one of the best hikes in RMNP. It requires 4.2 miles of moderately steep hiking, at altitude, up to 11,780 feet. The trail takes the hiker through woods and timberline to a true alpine setting: a beautiful deep lake in a spectacular mountain cirque at the base of the dramatic east face of Longs Peak. It doesn't get any better than that.

The hike begins at the Longs Peak ranger station (elevation 9,400 feet). Stop inside to see the exhibits: antique climbing hardware, the jacket of someone hit by lightning, and a model of Longs Peak and its surroundings. A kiosk outside warns that Longs Peak is a serious climb, unforgiving of the unwary and ill-prepared.

The hike offers a taste of many environments. Starting in montane forest, it climbs to sub-alpine forest, touches Alpine Brook several times, and is often adorned with beautiful wildflowers. The trail then rises through hardy, twisted trees—known as krummholz—to rocky tundra. The trail then crosses two areas that are steep snowfields in

Chasm Lake, at the base of Longs Peak, is remarkably deep.

PHOTO BY GORDON S. NOVAK JR.

early season, then enters a verdant high valley, and finally climbs a steep granite bench to the lake.

Opportunities for photography abound: wildflowers, wildlife (pikas, marmots, ptarmigan), and dramatic views of Mount Meeker, Mount Lady Washington, and of course Longs Peak. For best photography, start before 8 a.m., because the east face of Longs Peak will be in shadow by noon.

Expect to consume at least 2 quarts of water; probably a good deal more.

GETTING THERE: The road to the Longs Peak ranger station is located right at mile 9 on Colorado 7 (look for green mile markers beside the road), 9 miles south of Estes Park, or

Columbine Falls from Chasm Lake Trail.   PHOTO BY GORDON S. NOVAK JR.

about 25 miles from Lyons via Allenspark. Follow the road west several miles steeply uphill, and turn left at the top for the ranger station. Parking spaces may be scarce in the last half of summer.

THE ROUTE: The trail starts out climbing fairly steeply; it doesn't get any steeper than this, but later it will be at higher altitude. At 0.5 mile up the trail there is a branch off to the right toward Eugenia Mine and Estes Cone; the left branch, which you take, goes to Chasm Lake and Longs Peak. The trail soon turns left and after 0.5 mile reaches a good rest stop beside Alpine Brook—at about 30 minutes from the trailhead.

The trail turns back north, then switchbacks south and curves around to the west, now heading toward Longs Peak. It passes the Goblins Forest campsite (home of an occasional porcupine, if not goblin), then rejoins the stream for a set of six switchbacks. The small meadows here are filled with wildflowers in early season. Near the top of the switchbacks is a log footbridge over the creek and a sign warning of the dangers of lightning above timberline. This is a good second rest stop, at about 1.5 hours into your hike.

Snow may be seen just above this creek crossing in early season, because the trail rises above timberline and gains the ridge top. There is a good view of Twin Sisters to the east as well as Meeker, Longs, and Mount Lady Washington. The trail reverses to a trail junction for Jim's Grove (a last outpost of trees above timberline) near the creek.

The trail now heads toward Longs Peak and the point where the left slope of Mount Lady Washington meets Lightning Ridge (well named—don't hesitate to retreat if the weather turns bad). You will start to feel the altitude, and your pace will likely slow down. Look for marmots, pikas, and weasels along the trail.

At about 2.5 hours you reach Chasm Junction, where the trail splits—the left branch heading to Chasm Lake and the right to Boulderfield, Storm Peak, the Keyhole, and Longs Peak. Mount Lady Washington can be climbed directly from here as well. There's a rack for horses and llamas, and an open-air privy just up the ridge.

Marmots are here hoping for a handout; they will steal your sandwich out of your backpack if you let them. (It is a disservice to feed any animals in the park.)

Beyond the junction, the trail levels out. The lovely Peacock Pool lies in the valley below. Look up to the south for the Iron Gates—dramatic rock pillars guarding a rock couloir that is a route for climbing Mount Meeker. The trail clings to the side of Mount Lady Washington; stay on trail to avoid steep and slippery slopes to the south.

Early in the season, the trail crosses two steep snowfields with rocks below. An ice axe self-belay is handy if you brought your axe, but most hikers cross with no special equipment.

Columbine Falls flows over rock slabs at the entrance of Chasm Meadows, a lovely green valley with a stream flowing through it. A stone hut, shaped like the Ships Prow at the head of the valley, stores supplies for emergency rescues on Longs Peak. It replaces an older stone hut that was destroyed by an avalanche in 2003.

Chasm Lake lies to the right, enclosed by a massive granite wall. The start of the route around the lake is well marked; be careful of loose gravel and sometimes slippery rock. At the top of the rocks, you are struck by the beauty of Chasm Lake with the east face of Longs Peak rising dramatically above. There is no finer sight in the Park.

Return to the trailhead by retracing your steps.

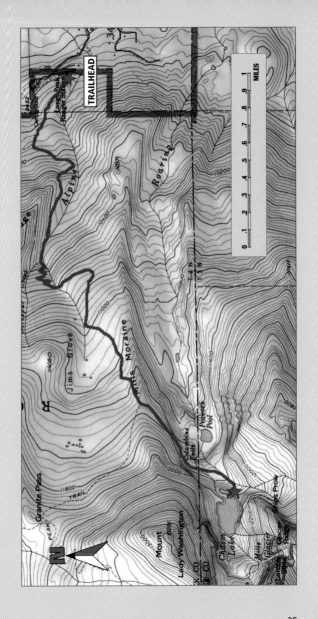

4. Cub Lake Trail

BY CHRISTIAN GREEN

MAPS	Trails Illustrated, Rocky Mountain National Park, Number 200 USGS, McHenrys Peak, Longs Peak Quadrangles, 7.5 minute
ELEVATION GAIN	690 feet
RATING	Easy–moderate
ROUND-TRIP DISTANCE	4.6 miles
ROUND-TRIP TIME	3 hours
NEAREST LANDMARK	Moraine Park Visitor Center

COMMENT: Cub Lake is one of those trails in Rocky Mountain National Park that can get quite crowded, even during a weekday in the fall. It's a popular year-round hike for families and tourists, so if you prefer to hike at a moderate to fast pace, be prepared to pass many casual hikers along the trail.

The trail is relatively level and short (2.3 miles to Cub Lake), until you reach the 1.75-mile mark, where the trail begins to climb toward the lake and becomes more moderate. Wildlife, including elk, abounds in Moraine Park, which lies just to the east of the first part of the trail. As you walk to the trailhead, don't be surprised if a car or two with out-of-state plates pulls over and the driver asks if you've seen any elk.

GETTING THERE: From Estes Park, continue on US 36 west to the Park entrance near Beaver Meadows Visitor Center. From there, drive 0.25 mile to Bear Lake Road and turn left. After travelling a little more than 0.1 mile, turn right and head toward Moraine Lake Campground and Fern Lake (the Moraine Lake Visitor Center will be on your left when you make this turn). After approximately 0.5 mile, make a left turn onto Fern Lake Road and follow the signs for the Fern Lake and Cub Lake trailheads. The parking lot for Cub Lake

The aspen grove along Cub Lake Trail.   PHOTO BY CHRISTIAN GREEN

Trail is a little more than 1.0 mile down Fern Lake Road. There is additional parking 0.2 mile past the main lot.

THE ROUTE: The trailhead is just west of the parking lot (or just east, if you park in the overflow lot). The trail may begin in marshland, depending on the time of year and flow of the Big Thompson River. A wooden bridge traverses the Big Thompson, which flows from Forest Canyon in the park all the way to about 5 miles south of Greeley, where it joins the South Platte River. After crossing the bridge, the first part of the trail is fairly level and winds its way past the western border of Moraine Park, where elk can often be spotted, particularly during the fall rutting season.

A key feature to this section of the trail is a series of large boulders lining the trail. Although this part of the trail is level, keep an eye out for rocks that can lead to a sprained ankle if your focus strays. The trail here is generally open, with coniferous trees, such as ponderosa pines and firs, dotting the landscape on either side.

Lily pads in Cub Lake.　　　　PHOTO BY JACK POWERS

Shortly after passing a series of small beaver ponds on the left, a little more than 1.0 mile into the hike, the trail becomes more wooded and rockier, as it begins to ascend toward Cub Lake. Around the 1.75-mile mark, the trail enters an aspen grove. The thick canopy of aspens makes this part of the trail a cool refuge during the summer months, and it serves as a portal to Cub Lake. Up to this point, the hike has been relatively easy; here it becomes moderate and rockier.

Just past the 2.0-mile mark, around where the Cub Creek Campsite crosstrail enters from the left, the trail begins to open up again. From this point, it's a short 0.1 mile jaunt to the northeast side of Cub Lake—the outlet for a stream that runs in an easterly direction from the lake. Although the lake is generally surrounded by trees, this area is fairly open and presents a photo opportunity of the lake, with Stones Peak (12,922 feet) and Sprague Mountain (12,713 feet) serving as a nice backdrop. The main trail continues above the lake for another 0.3 mile, until it intersects with Mill Creek Trail.

After heading up the trail a bit, look for a nice boulder along the northern shore where you can rest and grab a snack or lunch. During the summer and early fall, the lake is covered by lily pads and offers a serene setting to enjoy the site of mallard ducks gliding along the lake's surface or a Steller's jay foraging for seeds along the forest floor. Once you're finished eating and enjoying the pristine setting, head the 2.3 miles back down the trail to the parking lot. Perhaps you will be lucky enough to catch a glimpse of that elusive herd of elk the tourists have been searching for all morning.

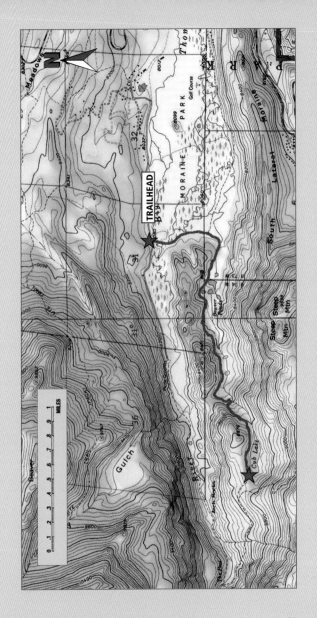

5. Deer Mountain Trail

BY JACK POWERS

MAPS	Trails Illustrated, Rocky Mountain National Park, Number 200 USGS, Estes Park Quadrangle 7.5 minute
ELEVATION GAIN	1,013 feet
RATING	Moderate
ROUND-TRIP DISTANCE	6 miles
ROUND-TRIP TIME	3 hours
NEAREST LANDMARK	Estes Park

COMMENT: At first glance, Deer Mountain can be intimidating, especially when viewed from the Fall River entrance. The mountain looms steep and massive above the road. Fortunately, the road continues to a trailhead well above the north base of the mountain. The climb is also mitigated by many switchbacks, which keep the incline to a moderate level.

You don't have to wait to gain the summit to enjoy the scenery. Impressive views of Upper Beaver Meadow, Moraine Park, and Longs Peak lie to the south. Equally fine views of Horseshoe Park and the peaks of the Mummy Range are to the northwest. The vistas are often the best at the switchbacks themselves.

Upon reaching the summit, you'll enjoy a panoramic view of nearly 360 degrees. In addition to the already-mentioned peaks and valleys, the summit offers unobstructed views of Hallett Peak and other peaks on the Continental Divide. Estes Park and Lake Estes can be seen to the east. Looking down on the Beaver Meadows entrance, where cars appear to be miniature toys, gives an appreciation of the height that you have reached and, as well, a good feeling of accomplishment.

Deer Mountain aspens, with Longs Peak in the background.

It should be noted that Deer Mountain stands off by itself and can be a target for lightning. You should descend immediately if threatening weather is observed.

GETTING THERE: The Deer Ridge trailhead is at the junction of US 34 and US 36. Parking spots are immediately to the east of this intersection along both sides of US 36.

US 34 enters the Park through the Fall River entrance. The trailhead is roughly 4 miles from the entrance. The route goes past Horseshoe Park and then climbs to the intersection with US 36.

US 36 enters the Park through the Beaver Meadows entrance. Drive past Bear Lake Road and continue uphill for 3 miles to the intersection with US 34. From this direction, the trailhead is a little before the intersection.

THE ROUTE: The trail initially heads to the east along Deer Ridge and then around to the west side of Deer Mountain. There is a junction with the North Deer Mountain Trail after 0.1 mile. Continue on the Deer Mountain Trail, which is to the right. After 0.8 mile, the trail comes to the first of many switchbacks. At this point, and downslope, there is a

Rustic trail to Deer Mountain. PHOTO BY JACK POWERS

grove of aspens. In the fall, these aspens make a great fore-ground for pictures of Longs Peak to the south.

The trail, after the first switchback, climbs gradually along a lightly wooded section on the west side of the mountain. Photographers might want to try their luck framing Ypsilon Mountain with two of the ponderosas alongside the trail.

The trail enters the forest after the second switchback and remains in shade until reaching the summit. The trail moves back and forth across the west side of the mountain, provid-ing alternating views of Horseshoe Park and Moraine Park.

Much of the mountain top is relatively flat, with only a couple of switchbacks after a slight downhill section among a mixture of aspens and conifers. The actual summit is reached by a 0.2-mile spur trail that is marked with a sign. The spur is the steepest part of the route, but any stops to catch your breath are done with the knowledge that the goal is close at hand.

The summit is on the south side of the mountain. It is flat, with room for many hikers. Randomly situated boulders can serve as benches. There are no retaining walls or fences, but the terrain is such that the view can be enjoyed and pictures taken without standing on the edge of a precipice.

Return to the trailhead by retracing your steps.

6. Emerald Lake Trail

BY KURT WORRELL

MAPS	Trails Illustrated, Rocky Mountain National Park, Number 200 USGS, McHenrys Peak Quadrangle 7.5 Minute
ELEVATION GAIN	673 feet, plus 413 feet spur to Haiyaha
RATING	Easy
ROUND-TRIP DISTANCE	3 miles
ROUND-TRIP TIME	2–3 hours
NEAREST LANDMARK	Estes Park to Bear Lake trailhead

COMMENT: The Bear Lake area is one of the main destinations for visitors to Rocky Mountain National Park. Situated 9,400 feet above sea level, the trailheads located at the west edge of the parking area provide access to a great many peaks and lakes.

The trails to Nymph, Dream, and Emerald lakes take you through pine forest, on the climbing sections of the trail, and aspen groves nearer the lakes.

The route from Nymph Lake to Dream Lake proceeds along a well-groomed, south-facing trail around the north and west edges of the lake and provides additional photo opportunities of the Longs Peak massif shortly after leaving the lake basin. Dream Lake offers excellent views of Hallett Peak and Flattop Mountain.

The trail to Emerald Lake skirts the north edge of Dream Lake as you pass its full length. At this point in the hike, the trail is well inside the canyon, with steep cliffs to the north (Flattop Mountain) and to the south (culminating at Hallett Peak). This can make for comfortable hiking during the hot summers, but the lack of direct sunlight early or late

Emerald Lake from Flattop Mountain Trail.　　PHOTO BY JACK POWERS

in the day can produce a chill in the air. This cold weather maintains the Tyndall Glacier, located about 1.25 miles west beyond Emerald Lake.

GETTING THERE: The Beaver Meadows entrance station is situated 1.4 miles west of the Beaver Meadows Visitors Center on US 36. From the entrance station, travel 0.3 mile on Trail Ridge Road and take the first left, following the signs to Bear Lake Road. You will pass the Moraine Park Museum and the turnoff to the campground after 1.3 miles. Continue along Bear Lake Road for another 4.4 miles to the Glacier Basin/Park & Ride crossroad. During high traffic times, a shuttle is run from the Park & Ride to all destinations farther along Bear Lake Road. A shuttle ride may be required if the Bear Lake parking lot is full. Plan to arrive at the trailhead before 7 a.m., if you want to avoid the traffic congestion and the potential shuttle ride. From the Park & Ride, continue along Bear Lake Road, passing the Glacier Gorge trailhead parking lot in 2.7 miles. The final 0.6 mile brings you to the Bear Lake trailhead parking lot. All trails are located at the west end of the parking lot.

THE ROUTE: Proceed to the west end of the Bear Lake parking lot. There you'll find the shuttle bus stop, pit toilets, and ranger station. As you pass the ranger station, you'll cross a large wooden bridge. Once across the bridge, the right path takes you to Bear Lake while the trail to the left leads to the standard Nymph/Dream/Emerald Lake Trail. Keep left. After a very short distance, the Glacier Gorge Junction Trail exits to the left. Keep to the right past the trail registry and continue for 0.5 mile to Nymph Lake. The gently climbing path traverses the north side of Chaos Creek, which is fed by both Dream Lake and Lake Haiyaha. The well-maintained trail begins in the pine forest but opens up roughly halfway to the lake, giving splendid views of Longs Peak and its neighbors. As the trail reenters the forest, it will turn northward and traverse along the east side of Nymph Lake. Continue north until you have reached the northern edge of Nymph Lake.

Follow the trail westward along the north side of Nymph Lake. As the trail rises it changes from dirt to rough blacktop. Continue until the trail turns south and heads directly toward Longs Peak. Several photo opportunities of Longs Peak appear once the trail turns to the west again and heads up the drainage. Continue west up the drainage until you reach a switchback. After ascending you will arrive at the outlet of Dream Lake. Keep right at the trail sign indicating Dream and Emerald lakes to the right (and Lake Haiyaha to the left). Shortly thereafter wooden bridges cross the stream and and the trail takes you directly to Dream Lake. Taking the trail down to the lake itself provides an excellent photo opportunity with Hallett Peak in the background.

From Dream Lake, follow the trail west along the north side of the lake to the inlet. From here, climb steadily on groomed trails of wood and rock steps into Tyndall Gorge. The terrain here is steep until the drainage levels out for the remaining stroll to the outlet of Emerald Lake.

Return by backtracking to Dream, Nymph, and Bear lakes.

7. Fern Lake Trail

BY ALAN APT

MAPS	Trails Illustrated, Rocky Mountain National Park, Number 200
ELEVATION GAIN	2,900 feet (starting at 9,475 feet)
RATING	Moderate–difficult
ROUND-TRIP DISTANCE	5–10 miles
ROUND-TRIP TIME	4–8 hours
NEAREST LANDMARK	Bear Lake trailhead

COMMENT: This pristine, sparkling lake can be reached from either the Cub Lake trailhead, in Moraine Park, or the Bear Lake trailhead. The Bear Lake route is more challenging, but rewards the ambitious with spectacular scenery from beginning to end, and is a rewarding mountaineering experience.

From Bear Lake, the trail ascends quickly, offering stunning views of 14,259-foot Longs Peak, Hallett Peak, and magical Glacier Gorge. After climbing 1,100 feet up to Lake Helene, you'll see the spectacle of Notchtop, Little Matterhorn, and Gabletop mountains soaring above you across the gorge. The fun thousand-foot descent to picturesque Fern Lake then begins; however, you will have to make this up on your return jaunt to Lake Helene. If you prefer a nice, more moderate hike, reverse your course after reaching Lake Helene or Odessa Lake. These options are the reason for the variations in the rating, distance, and time noted above.

GETTING THERE: From Estes Park, enter Rocky Mountain National Park on US 36; go through the Beaver Meadows entrance, and in about 0.25 mile take the first left turn onto Bear Lake Road. In approximately 3.0 miles you'll arrive at the shuttle bus parking lot across from the Glacier Basin

Fern Lake.

campground. The Bear Lake trailhead and parking lot is less than 3.0 miles farther on. In order to relieve congestion at the trailhead, and to cut down on vehicle emissions in the park, it is recommended that you ride the comfortable and free shuttle bus.

THE ROUTE: Go to the information booth at the Bear Lake trailhead. From there, bear right to Bear Lake and take the obligatory photos of magnificent Hallett Peak towering above the lake. Go counterclockwise around the lake for about 100 yards and look for the signage that will take you to the Fern Lake and Flattop Mountain trails. Go right, uphill, and bear left in approximately 0.25 mile at the first intersection, where the trail splits off to Bierstadt Lake. If it's a clear day, about 200 yards uphill beyond that point you will enjoy the gorgeous panorama of Longs Peak and Glacier Gorge, to the southeast.

In about 0.5 mile, when the Flattop Mountain Trail turns left (west), continue straight (northwest). You will enter trees now and have intermittent views to the east as you climb steadily and gradually past the northeast flank of Flattop Mountain.

Fern Lake Trail—The Pool.

PHOTO BY JACK POWERS

The trail eventually emerges from the trees and steepens as it veers southwest, and then north, past Lake Helene (10,600 feet) at the 3.0-mile mark, and then goes down to Odessa Lake (10,055 feet).

The massif to the west of Notchtop, Little Matterhorn, and Gabletop mountains is a visual treat that is on a par with the Alps of Europe. The trail then steeply descends to and past Odessa Lake, and then, finally, all the way down another 1.0 mile to the sparkling waters of Fern Lake (9,503 feet).

If you have arranged a car shuttle, you can continue downhill to the Cub Lake trailhead. It is a more picturesque and challenging mountaineering adventure, however, to retrace your steps back to Bear Lake.

Editor's note: Alan Apt is the author of *Snowshoe Routes, Colorado's Front Range*, 2E, a Colorado Mountain Club Press publication, and *Afoot and Afield in Denver/Boulder & Colorado's Front Range*.

8. Finch Lake

BY GORDON S. NOVAK JR.

MAPS	Trails Illustrated, Rocky Mountain National Park, Number 200 USGS, Allenspark Quadrangle 7.5 Minute
ELEVATION GAIN	1,442 feet
RATING	Moderate
ROUND-TRIP DISTANCE	9 miles
ROUND-TRIP TIME	4–5 hours
NEAREST LANDMARK	Allenspark

COMMENT: Finch Lake is a peaceful and beautiful lake with plentiful wildlife. This hike is green and woodsy, with mountains in the distance, as opposed to the rocky hikes into the mountains. Many people fish at Finch Lake.

The hike begins with a long ascent up a ramp on the eastern edge of the ridge on the south side of Wild Basin. Then it turns east, through varied forests, toward Finch Lake. A few breaks in the trees provide good views of Mount Meeker and Chiefs Head Peak. From here, Dragon's Egg Rock (actually a cliff band) looks a bit like an egg.

The lush forest supports a variety of wildlife, from snowshoe hares to bighorn sheep, and possibly bears, cougars, and moose. Deer and elk, however, are more likely to be seen. When I arrived at the lake, deer were grazing on the far side in early evening, creating a peaceful and charming scene.

GETTING THERE: The trailhead is inside the Wild Basin entrance to RMNP. The entrance is at about mile 13 on Highway 7 (look for green mile markers beside the road), about 13 miles south of Estes Park, or 2 miles north of Allenspark.

Finch Lake, with Elk Tooth in the background.   PHOTO BY GORDON S. NOVAK JR.

Coming from Denver and the east via Lyons, the Allenspark route (left turn out of Lyons) will be shorter. The entrance is at a valley bottom containing the North St. Vrain Creek. Once past the entrance station, follow the road toward the Wild Basin ranger station for about 1.0 mile, where you will find a small parking area and trailhead on the left side; if you get to the ranger station, you've gone too far.

THE ROUTE: The route is straightforward from the trailhead, with only a side branch to Allenspark along the way. Once you reach Finch Lake there are a variety of options. The trail continues on to Pear Lake and is well worth the longer hike. Fishermen love Pear Lake and many will bushwhack 1.0 mile southeast to try their luck in a high stream—Pear Lake is also a starting point for climbing Elk Tooth. A nearby stable rents horses and you may encounter some on your trek to Finch Lake. Note: horses on the trail always have the right of way. Experienced,

Pagoda Mountain, Longs Peak, and Mount Meeker from Finch Lake Trail.
PHOTO BY GORDON S. NOVAK JR

polite hikers will move to the uphill portion of a sloping trail, hold their trekking poles still, and speak quietly to the riders.

There is an alternate return route via a trail to Calypso Cascades, then down via the Wild Basin ranger station trailhead. Be aware though that this leaves you 1.0 mile above the Finch Lake trailhead; you can take two cars and leave one there, bum a ride, or walk 1.0 mile down a dusty road with often heavy car traffic. Despite this mismatch in trailheads, the circle route provides multiple destinations and a scenic hike down the North St. Vrain creek.

Your alternative is to return to the trailhead by retracing your original steps.

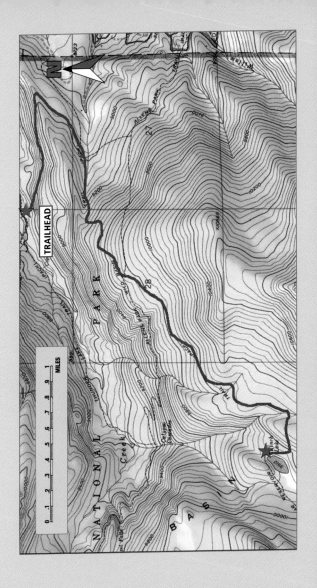

9. Flattop Mountain Trail

BY JACK POWERS

MAPS	Trails Illustrated, Rocky Mountain National Park, Number 200 USGS, McHenrys Peak Quadrangle 7.5 minute
ELEVATION GAIN	2,849 feet
RATING	Difficult
ROUND-TRIP DISTANCE	8.8 miles
ROUND-TRIP TIME	5 hours
NEAREST LANDMARK	Estes Park

COMMENT: Flattop Mountain is a popular trail that takes the hiker to a summit on the Continental Divide. The trail, which starts at Bear Lake, is forested along the first two-thirds of its length and then emerges into tundra for the final climb to the summit. It passes dramatic overlooks for both Dream and Emerald lakes along the way.

The forested area gradually changes with elevation. The tall and dense trees at the lower elevations yield to smaller trees and finally to krummholz, a German word which translates as crooked or twisted wood. Krummholz occurs at higher elevations and is a result of exposure to harsh natural elements.

The open tundra gives the hiker a 360-degree panorama of neighboring peaks and lower lying lakes. Bierstadt and Sprague lakes can be seen far below to the east. Notchtop Mountain, Little Matterhorn, and the Gable are to the north. Longs Peak, the Keyboard of the Winds, and Pagoda Mountain dominate the view to the south. And, immediately to the west, the challenging climb to the summit of Flattop is visible. The summit is at 12,324 feet, and folks who are not acclimated to high elevations are advised to test themselves on less strenuous trails before trying this hike.

Otis, Hallett, and Flattop peaks from Lake Bierstadt.   PHOTO BY JACK POWERS

GETTING THERE: The Flattop Mountain hike starts at Bear Lake. Drive to the Beaver Meadows entrance to Rocky Mountain National Park, on US 36, and take the first left turn onto Bear Lake Road. It is about 0.25 mile from the toll booths. Proceed approximately 9 miles to the Bear Lake parking lot at the end of the road.

During high season, the Bear Lake parking lot may fill by mid-morning. The Glacier Gorge Park & Ride is a convenient and greener alternative. The bus system also will provide an alternative when there are construction delays or closures. Check at the Visitors Center or the Park website for traffic alerts.

THE ROUTE: The hike starts at Bear Lake. Turn right and go along the loop trail for 90 yards. Then turn right onto the trail to Flattop and other locations. There are signs and an information kiosk at that point. The trail climbs through aspens and evergreens for about 0.33 mile and then comes

Among the clouds on Flattop Mountain.   PHOTO BY WARD LUTHI

to another junction. Turn left—it is a sharp left—at this point, and continue to climb. The last junction comes after another 0.4 mile. Again, turn left.

The next point of interest will be the Dream Lake overlook. This is a good place to stop and enjoy the view of Dream Lake roughly 570 feet below. After the Dream Lake overlook, the trail continues to climb with multiple switchbacks. Eventually you reach the region of krummholz and some flag trees. Flag trees have branches only on the side of the trunk that is out of the fierce prevailing winds.

The Emerald Lake overlook is virtually at the tree line. It is a good place to stop and look down on Emerald Lake and the depth of the Tyndall Gorge. After the overlook, the trail travels through rocks and tundra. You may see ptarmigans, pikas, and marmots here. Flowers do bloom here, but don't expect tall stalks. The trail gets smoother and more gradual as the summit gets closer. This is good because the air is noticeably thinner.

Not surprisingly, Flattop is flat on the top and there is no official marker for the summit. The highest point is somewhere in the area of the route that many hikers take on their way to neighboring Hallett Peak. Others stop at the point where the Flattop Trail terminates at the junction with The Inlet and Tonahutu Creek trails. There are many spectacular views from the summit. Take care not to go too close to precipices as you explore the summit region.

Return to the trailhead by retracing your steps.

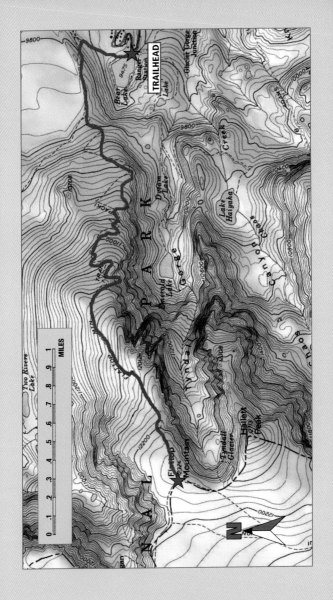

10. Lion Lake Trail

BY SALLIE VARNER

MAPS	Trails Illustrated, Rocky Mountain National Park, Number 200
ELEVATION GAIN	3,050 feet
RATING	Difficult
ROUND-TRIP DISTANCE	13.3/14.9 miles
ROUND-TRIP TIME	7–10 hours
NEAREST LANDMARK	Wild Basin turnoff from Hwy 7

COMMENT: The hike to Lion Lakes No. 1 and No. 2 and Snowbank Lake is long and has a good deal of elevation gain, but it is well worth your effort. The lakes are in a stunning setting—a high alpine bowl with Mount Alice, the Continental Divide, and Chiefs Head Peak looming above. While Lion Lake No. 1 may be the prettiest of the three, hikers will enjoy the fun, easy scramble beside Trio Falls to reach Lion Lake No. 2 and the short tundra ramble to Snowbank Lake.

GETTING THERE: This hike starts from the Wild Basin trailhead south of Estes Park. From the junction of US 34 and US 36 on the west side of Estes Park, drive south on US 36 for nearly 0.5 mile to the junction with Colorado 7. Take the right fork onto Hwy 7 and follow it for 12.8 miles, to the well-marked turnoff for Wild Basin. Watch for outstanding views of Longs Peak and Mount Meeker as you travel south of Estes. Turn right at the Wild Basin turnoff, pass through the Rocky Mountain National Park entrance station, and drive west on the good dirt road for 2.6 miles, to the large Wild Basin parking area at the end of the road.

This trailhead offers pit toilets and trash cans and also houses a National Park ranger station.

Arriving at Lion Lakes. PHOTO BY SALLIE VARNER

THE ROUTE: Follow the Wild Basin Trail west from the parking area toward Ouzel Falls and Thunder Lake for 1.3 miles to the junction with the trail leading to Tahosa, Aspen Knoll, Siskin, and North St. Vrain campsites. If you turn at the junction onto this steeper, narrower side trail to the campsites, you benefit from a slight shortcut—at the cost of missing Calypso Cascades and Ouzel Falls. It rejoins the main trail after 1.2 miles, at a signed junction 0.6 mile above Ouzel Falls, after saving about 0.8 mile from the main trail.

Hikers who prefer to follow the main trail will cross North St. Vrain Creek shortly after passing the campsites trail, and continue west past Calypso Cascades, Ouzel Falls, and the turnoff for Ouzel and Bluebird Lakes to the upper end of the campsites trail, 3.3 miles from the trailhead. From this junction, follow the Thunder Lake Trail 1.3 miles to the signed Lion Lakes Trail.

The Lion Lakes Trail starts with a very steep climb and continues to climb steeply for nearly 1.0 mile, then moderates slightly with more gradual up and down grades. Pass through some high meadows before the final short descent

Hard Rock Hiker at Lion Lakes. PHOTO BY SALLIE VARNER

to Lion Lake No. 1, just over 2 miles from the junction with the Thunder Lake Trail.

To continue to Lion Lake No. 2, follow the trail along the east side of the lake. After crossing the small creek that flows into the lake from the north, the trail fades quickly. Almost immediately you will cross a second, smaller creek, then follow cairns and faded bits of trail across large rock faces and through stands of pine trees. Head generally toward Trio Falls, which can be seen descending the large rock face to the west. A third creek crossing can be made in several places, lower or higher, so that the final approach to Trio Falls is along the south side of the creek.

Scramble up the rock face to the left of Trio Falls. There are many possible routes for this short climb, some marked with cairns. The easiest and most direct route is at a small notch in the cliff on the left (south) side of the falls. Follow cairns above the falls to find your way through stands of junipers and over rocks to Lion Lake No. 2, 0.6 mile above Lion Lake No. 1.

For the final short hike to Snowbank Lake, pass Lion Lake No. 2 along the south (left) shore and continue following cairns through more junipers for 0.25 mile to this high lake.

Retrace your steps to return to the original trailhead.

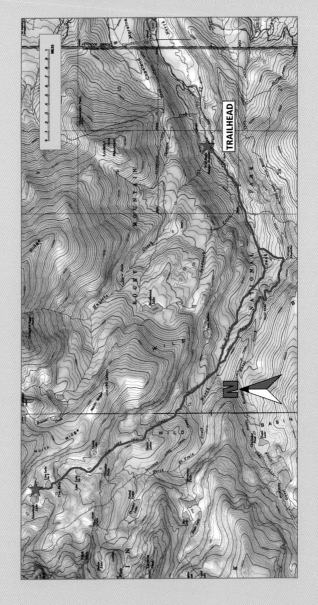

TRAILHEAD

11. Lone Pine Lake

BY GORDON S. NOVAK JR.

MAPS	Trails Illustrated, Rocky Mountain National Park, Number 200 USGS, Isolation Park Quadrangle 7.5 Minute
ELEVATION GAIN	1,500 feet
RATING	Moderate
ROUND-TRIP DISTANCE	11 miles
ROUND-TRIP TIME	5–6 hours
NEAREST LANDMARK	Grand Lake

COMMENT: Lone Pine Lake is named for a small rock island within the lake, with a picturesque tree growing on it. The lake lies below timberline in a lovely steep-sided valley. This valley carries the East Inlet Creek, one of several that feed Grand Lake, the headwaters of the Colorado River.

The trail passes by Adams Falls, 0.3 mile from the trailhead, a spot well worth pausing at for the view. It then curves around to the north, skirting a swampy flat area with the creek curving through it. Keep an eye out for the plentiful wildlife, including moose, as well as a variety of wildflowers.

While this area was uniformly lush and green in the early years of this century, it has since suffered the loss of many trees due to warming and the Mountain Pine Beetle—factors that affect much of the Grand Lake area.

The open valley provides good views of Mount Craig, the mountain that dominates the view from Grand Lake. Because the trail follows the creek up the valley, drinking water is available (purify it, of course), and there are some nice views of the creek and small waterfalls. It is clear, though, that the trail builders sometimes had to route the

Lone Pine Lake—East Inlet Valley.   PHOTO BY GORDON S. NOVAK JR.

trail away from the creek and use dynamite to create a walkable path.

The lake offers numerous lovely spots for a snack or picnic lunch and a refuge to contemplate the beauty of the signature lone pine growing out of the rock island.

There are several popular campsites near Lone Pine Lake, and a high camp here offers access to numerous more ambitious hikes. Hikers who have made the trek to Lone Pine Lake can hike on to four more lakes: Lake Verna, Spirit Lake, Fourth Lake, and Fifth Lake. The valley is flanked by Andrews Peak, on the north, and Mount Craig, on the south. For a bold cross-country tour, climb past Fourth Lake to Boulder-Grand Pass, bagging Mount Alice and Tanima Peak on the way, and go down to Thunder Lake and out to Wild Basin.

GETTING THERE: Lone Pine Lake is reached via the East Inlet Trail, which begins at Grand Lake. Grand Lake is located on US 34 and can be reached via Trail Ridge Road, or from

A small waterfall along the trail.

PHOTO BY GORDON S. NOVAK JR.

Winter Park via Hwy 40 and Interstate 70.

From the entrance to the town of Grand Lake, follow Grand Avenue through town, then either continue on Grand Avenue or turn left onto West Portal Road as it curves to the right around the lake to the east side. There is an obvious unpaved parking lot at the trailhead.

THE ROUTE: The trail is clearly defined and easy to follow. There is a short side loop to Adams Falls, 0.3 mile from the trailhead; turn right upon rejoining the main trail. Aside from an initial broad turn to the north, to skirt a swampy area, the trail heads east. Getting lost is almost impossible: any route back down the valley will return to Grand Lake. Some sections of trail appear to be made from dynamited rubble, making these sections even rockier than usual. After Lone Pine Lake, the trail becomes progressively less distinct until it may disappear altogether. At this point, retrace your steps back west toward Grand Lake. The East Inlet valley points straight at the town of Grand Lake, so that line-of-sight cell phone reception may be possible at certain points along the trail.

Editor's note: Moose, which were re-introduced to our state not that many years ago, can often be seen in the marshy area beyond Adams Falls. Although they are exciting to view, some experts depict them as the most dangerous animal in Colorado—mostly because of their immense size, unpredictability, and occasionally aggressive behavior. The most dangerous moose encounter would be to approach a mother with a calf. As with other wild game, moose are best observed from a reasonable distance.

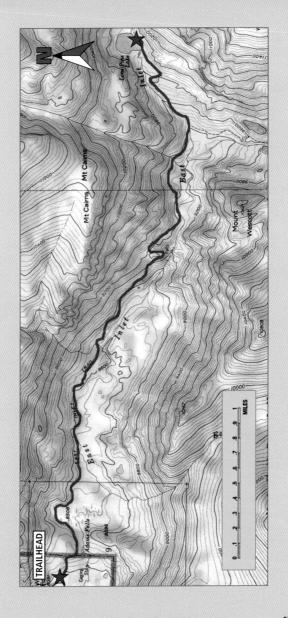

LONE PINE LAKE   67

12. Longs Peak—Keyhole Route

BY CAROLINE BLACKWELL SCHMIEDT
AND RUDY SCHMIEDT

MAPS	Trails Illustrated, Rocky Mountain National Park, Number 200 USGS, Longs Peak Quadrangle 7.5 Minute
ELEVATION GAIN	4,859 feet
RATING	Difficult and strenuous
ROUND-TRIP DISTANCE	15 miles
ROUND-TRIP TIME	10–14 hours
NEAREST LANDMARK	Estes Park

COMMENT: Longs Peak has attracted adventurous souls to its summit for more than 100 years. It is the highest and most prominent feature within Rocky Mountain National Park. Longs Peak is named after Major Stephen Long, who, although an early explorer in the 1820s, never climbed to the summit. The first recorded ascent of Longs Peak was in 1868 by a party led by geologist and explorer John Wesley Powell. It is likely, however, that Native Americans climbed to the summit much earlier, trapping eagles for their feathers. In 1873, Isabella Bird was one of the first women to climb Longs Peak. She described the climb in her book *A Lady's Life in the Rocky Mountains*. The famous naturalist Enos Mills, influential in the establishment of Rocky Mountain National Park, led many climbers to the summit, including 8-year-old Harriet Peters in 1905.

Longs Peak is a challenging climb and should not be attempted without adequate preparation. A high level of fitness is required to safely complete a Longs Peak ascent. Several areas along the route beyond the Keyhole are particularly difficult, with worn slippery rock surfaces and significant exposure. In one such spot, the polite gesture of

Longs Peak.

stepping aside to give another climber more space proved fatal for a Park visitor. Someone dies almost every year while climbing Longs Peak. Extreme caution must be exercised at all times.

Don't hesitate to constantly assess risk factors—particularly in regard to climbers' physical well-being and weather conditions. Watch yourself and your companions for such altitude sickness indicators as headaches or nausea. Be alert to changes in the weather—especially rain or snow. Good places to take such assessments include the beginning of the Boulder Field and the Keyhole. Don't hesitate to retreat if the situation warrants it.

Proper gear, including sturdy hiking boots, waterproof clothing, headlamp, sunscreen, backpack, and adequate food and water, is essential. A helmet is also recommended beyond the Keyhole. The route is considered "technical" during most of the year, due to the presence of ice and snow. Late summer offers optimal trail conditions. Local guide services are available in Estes Park.

GETTING THERE: From the junction of US 36 and Colorado 7 in Estes Park, drive south on Colorado 7 for 8.8 miles to the Longs Peak trailhead entrance. Turn right and continue 1.0 mile to the trailhead parking lot and ranger station.

THE ROUTE: Stop at the trailhead and take a look at the Longs Peak kiosk. Just beyond the kiosk is a trail register. It is a good idea to sign in here, identifying yourself, the number of people in your party, the time you began your hike, and your anticipated destination, route, and return time.

Any day hike of Longs Peak (i.e., one that does not involve camping overnight at the boulder field) should begin in the early morning hours, around 1 to 3 a.m. An early start is necessary in order to reach the summit and descend back below timberline before afternoon thunderstorms begin. Because you will be hiking in the dark for several hours, a headlamp is required. Consider carrying a backup light source and extra batteries.

From the trail register, the trail climbs steadily through the forest for 0.5 mile to the junction of the trail to Eugenia Mine and Estes Cone, which veers to the right. Continue through this junction, climbing steadily to a bridge crossing Alpine Brook. Shortly after the bridge, the trail ascends above timberline, crossing through a forest of short twisted trees. From here, the trail climbs to the southwest, following Mills Moraine, a prominent ridge. The trail continues to the junction with the Chasm Lake Trail, which is at the base of Mount Lady Washington. This spot affords stunning views of The Diamond on the east face of Longs Peak. Veer right at this junction and contour along the base

Longs Peak—the highest point in Rocky Mountain National Park.

PHOTO BY RUDY SCHMIEDT

of Mount Lady Washington, to the northwest toward Granite Pass.

Just beyond Granite Pass, continue on past the junction with the North Longs Peak Trail. The trail then winds up a series of switchbacks before reaching the Boulder Field, 5.9 miles from the trailhead. As the name implies, the Boulder Field is a large area strewn with boulders. It is nestled between Mount Lady Washington, Longs Peak, and Storm Peak. The trail ends here and you must climb over enormous boulders, working your way toward a prominent gap in the rocks—called the Keyhole—between Longs Peak and Storm Peak.

As you approach the Keyhole, you will notice a small stone hut, shaped like a beehive, to your left. This hut was constructed in memory of Agnes Vaille, a climber who died on the mountain in 1925. Be aware that, once you pass through the Keyhole, the character of the route changes significantly. You will no longer be hiking, you will be climbing and your pace will be much slower. The final distance of approximately 1.25 miles consists of four segments: the Ledges, the Trough, the Narrows, and the Homestretch.

From the Keyhole, the route is marked by red and yellow circles painted onto rocks (these resemble fried eggs). You are climbing on 1.4-billion-year-old Silver Plume granite, which has numerous large feldspar crystals. Ascend an inclined gully made slick over the years by numerous hiking boots. Two bolts in the rock provide good holds at a particularly exposed spot in the Ledges section. Soon, you descend 100-150 vertical feet down into the Trough. This descent, which must be climbed on your return, makes the true total climb of Longs Peak closer to 5,100 vertical feet. The Trough is long and exhausting but brings you about 700 vertical feet closer to the summit. In early to mid-July an ice axe may be helpful here. At the top of the Trough you must scramble, hand-over-hand, up a 20-foot near-vertical incline, perhaps the most technically difficult part of your ascent. Most people climb straight up the crack here, but a less direct and perhaps easier route is present just to the left. This may require some route finding.

The Narrows lie above this cliff. This section is very exposed, but made easier by numerous excellent rocky hand- and foot-holds. The views of Chiefs Head Peak and Wild Basin, far below, are spectacular. Continue climbing over ledges to the start of the Homestretch, a steep incline leading to the summit. The 14,000-foot elevation, plus the smooth, polished nature of the granite here, makes this final section seem to take longer. Be very careful here under wet or icy conditions. Once atop the Homestretch, the large, relatively flat summit of Longs Peak is yours. Return via the route described.

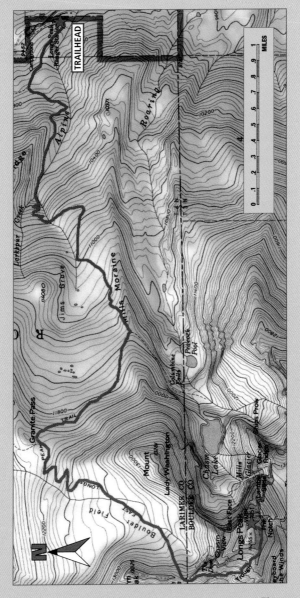

LONGS PEAK—KEYHOLE ROUTE

13. Lulu City Trail

BY AMY CROW

MAPS	Trails Illustrated, Rocky Mountain National Park, Number 200 USGS, Fall River Pass Quadrangle 7.5 minute
ELEVATION GAIN	350 feet
RATING	Easy
ROUND-TRIP DISTANCE	7.4 miles
ROUND-TRIP TIME	3 hours
NEAREST LANDMARK	Visitor Center, Trail Ridge Road

COMMENT: This easy and pleasant trip to the site of Lulu City is one that hikers of all ages can enjoy. The trail is well maintained and offers views of the Never Summer Range, including Lead Mountain, Tepee Mountain, and Mount Richthofen.

The dream of wealth created this transient mining town after silver was discovered in 1879 by prospector Joe Shipler. The town was built in 1880, with the backing of Benjamin F. Burnett and rancher William Baker, both of Fort Collins. Burnett's daughter, Lulu, was the namesake.

The town eventually grew to 40 cabins and a number of businesses. Ruins of some of these can still be seen. Although the silver proved to be low grade, and the town was rather quickly abandoned, Joe Shipler remained there another 30 years. The remains of Shipler's mine are 2 miles from the trailhead. On September 14, 1977, this site was placed on the National Register of Historic Places.

The natural beauty of this area is enhanced by the Colorado River, which runs peacefully alongside the trail. It's hard to believe that this river, little more than a stream and

Lulu City Trail, along the Colorado River.   PHOTO BY DANIELLE RAKER POOLE

miles away from the Grand Canyon, helped form one of Earth's great natural wonders.

Because of the ease of this trail, hikers can spend additional time at the site of Lulu City in the Kawuneeche Valley, with the sentinel Never Summers looking on.

GETTING THERE: From Estes Park, enter Rocky Mountain National Park at the Beaver Meadows entrance and drive 21.8 miles on Trail Ridge Road to the Alpine Visitor Center. (Trail Ridge Road begins on Hwy 36 but continues along Hwy 34.) Continue 10.7 miles from the Visitor Center to the Colorado River trailhead. The parking lot is off the highway and has toilet facilities. If you are coming from Grand Lake, the trailhead is approximately 10 miles almost due north of the Grand Lake entrance to the park.

Remnants of Shipler Mine.

PHOTO BY DANIELLE RAKER POOLE

THE ROUTE: The trail begins in a wooded area and is soon joined by the Colorado River, which is right along the trail at times. The grade is level for the 2 miles to the Shipler Mine, sometimes opening up to outstanding views of the Never Summers. This stretch is especially nice on a fall day when the leaves, ground cover, and grasses turn a multitude of colors.

Some structural remains can be explored at the Shipler Mine, which opens onto a meadow. (As with all other places in the Park, souvenir hunting is not allowed.)

The trail then heads back into the woods; here you will find a wilderness privy. Your hike continues along the old stage road that used to run through Lulu City. The trail splits to La Poudre Pass, 3.5 miles from the trailhead. Most of the elevation gain occurs in the last 2 miles to Lulu City, in a series of switchbacks. When the area levels into a meadow, the cobbled Colorado River once again joins the trail. At the Lulu City site, the sky opens up and you'll enjoy wonderful views of the Never Summer's painted peaks.

Retrace your steps to return to the trailhead.

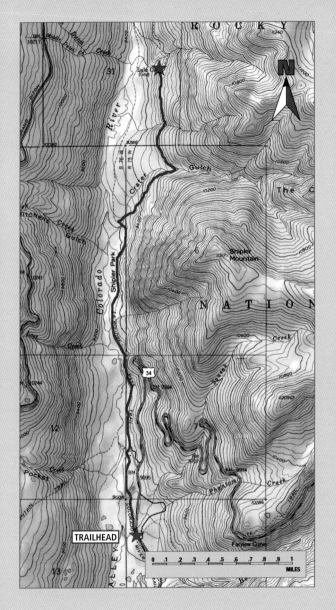

TRAILHEAD

14. Mills Lake Trail

BY CAROLINE BLACKWELL SCHMIEDT

MAPS	Trails Illustrated, Rocky Mountain National Park, Number 200 USGS, McHenrys Peak Quadrangle 7.5 Minute
ELEVATION GAIN	760 feet
RATING	Easy
ROUND-TRIP DISTANCE	5.6 miles
ROUND-TRIP TIME	4 hours
NEAREST LANDMARK	Estes Park

COMMENT: If you only have time to do one hike in Rocky Mountain National Park, you must hike to Mills Lake. This spectacular destination is considered one of the most scenic places within the park. Named after the famous naturalist Enos Mills, who was influential in the establishment of Rocky Mountain National Park, the hike is easy and suitable for families with school-aged children. Along the way you will pass beautiful Alberta Falls, which for many is a destination all to itself.

Nestled in the heart of Glacier Gorge, Mills Lake offers some of the most magnificent views found anywhere in the Park. Dramatic cliffs tower over the lake on two sides, while some of the highest peaks in the Park stand as sentinels in the distance. From the broad flat summit of Longs Peak, a ridge of unusual spires, called the Keyboard of the Winds, stretches to the southwest toward Pagoda Mountain. The name "Keyboard of the Winds" derives from the eerie sounds made by the wind as it channels through these landforms.

Glacier Gorge is a classic example of a U-shaped valley carved by glaciers. Evidence of glaciation abounds here. Look for large solitary boulders that appear to have been randomly placed where they rest. These boulders, called

Mills Lake—alpine splendor.

erratics, were left behind by receding glacial ice. Flat rock surfaces show evidence of glacial polish, grooves, and striations. These features were created by rocks and debris locked at the base of a glacier, which ground the valley floor as the ice moved past.

GETTING THERE: From the junction of US 34 and US 36 in Estes Park, continue west on US 36 4 miles to the Beaver Meadows entrance to Rocky Mountain National Park. From the entrance, continue 0.1 mile west to the junction with Bear Lake Road. Turn left on Bear Lake Road and drive 8.3 miles to the Glacier Gorge trailhead parking lot. If this parking lot is full, continue on to the Bear Lake parking lot, and then hike downhill 0.5 mile from Bear Lake to the Mills Lake Trail junction.

THE ROUTE: The trailhead is located on the south side of the Glacier Gorge parking lot. Stop here for a moment to look at the Glacier Gorge kiosk. The trail begins to the right of this kiosk. Follow the trail 0.3 mile to the junction with

Yoga at Mills Lake.   PHOTO BY WARD LUTHI

Bear Lake Trail. Turn left at this junction and follow the trail through a small grove of aspen trees. You will then pass over two log bridges before reaching Alberta Falls. In winter, the snowshoeing trail veers to the right between these two log bridges.

From Alberta Falls, the trail climbs steadily to the junction with the North Longs Peak Trail. Veer right here and continue on the trail as it hugs the side of a deep gorge above Glacier Creek, offering nice views of high peaks in the distance. From here the trail levels out a bit before reaching the junction with trails to Loch Vale and Lake Haiyaha. Veer left at this junction and follow the sign to Mills Lake.

Just past the junction, the trail passes a hitching rack before crossing a log bridge over Icy Brook. The trail then climbs steeply up a series of stone steps, crosses another log bridge, and climbs farther to an area characterized by flat, glacially scoured rock surfaces. Look here for glacial erratic boulders. If you find one, place your hand underneath it and feel the smooth rock surface upon which it rests. Notice how the presence of the boulder protects the glacially polished surface beneath it from weathering.

Follow a series of cairns across the glacially scoured terrain a short distance to the lake. From Mills Lake, consider hiking 2.2 miles farther, first past Jewel Lake and then on to Black Lake.

Return by retracing the route described.

TRAILHEAD

Prospect Canyon

Bear Lake

Ranger Station

Nymph Lake

Glacier Gorge Junction

Alberta Falls

KNOBE

NORTH

LONGS PEAK

TUNNEL

TRAIL TRACK

ADAMS

Glacier

HIGH VALE

Glacier Falls

GLACIER

Mills Lake

Jewel Lake

Half Mtn

Glacier

N

15. Ouzel Lake

BY JACK POWERS

MAPS	Trails Illustrated, Rocky Mountain National Park, Number 200 USGS, McHenrys Peak & Isolation Peak Quadrangles 7.5 minute
ELEVATION GAIN	1,510 feet
RATING	Moderate
ROUND-TRIP DISTANCE	9.8 miles
ROUND-TRIP TIME	5 hours
NEAREST LANDMARK	Estes Park

COMMENT: There are few hikes in Rocky Mountain National Park that include such a variety of features as the one to Ouzel Lake. The route includes several miles of subalpine forest, a high open ridge with commensurate vistas, waterfalls, cascades, and rapids. The final destination is a peaceful and picturesque lake whose valley is defined by three peaks.

An added bonus is that hikers need not go all the way to the lake to have a satisfying experience. The first set of waterfalls is only 0.3 mile from the trailhead. North St. Vrain Creek can be enjoyed for 1.4 miles before crossing the creek and climbing an additional 0.4 mile to Calypso Cascades. Ouzel Falls is 2.7 miles from the trailhead. Thus, the trail can be equally enjoyed by the novice and by seasoned hikers.

GETTING THERE: Ouzel Lake is in a southern section of the Park known as Wild Basin. The entrance to Wild Basin is off Colorado 7, roughly 12.7 miles south of the junction of Colorado 7 and US 36 in Estes Park. It is about 2.2 miles north of Allenspark on Colorado 7.

Ouzel Lake Trail.

PHOTO BY JACK POWERS

A sign marks where to turn west onto a county road. The actual entrance to the Park is a right turn about 0.4 mile down the county road. It is then a drive of about 2.2 miles along a dirt road from the fee station to the Wild Basin ranger station and parking lot. This is the summer parking lot; in winter the road is blocked 1.0 mile from the entrance.

THE ROUTE: Depending upon the information source, the initial section of the route is called either the Wild Basin Trail or the Thunder Lake Trail. Regardless of the name, the trail starts at the south side of the parking lot and immediately goes into a wooded area. The path is relatively smooth at this point and the inclines are gentle, as it passes near North St. Vrain Creek. After 0.3 mile, Lower Copeland Falls can be reached by taking a short spur trail to the creekside.

After leaving the lower falls, you have a choice of the main trail or a parallel trail that goes more directly to the Upper Copeland Falls. Both trails will get you to the upper falls, but the parallel trail offers the photographer more opportunities. The upper falls are only a few hundred yards from the lower.

Ouzel Falls.

PHOTO BY CAROLINE SCHMIEDT

The trail then climbs gradually along North St. Vrain Creek for the next 1.0 mile. The creek flow can be rapid and picturesque. Be aware, however, that it can also be dangerous. It doesn't take many inches of rapidly flowing water to sweep a grown person off his or her feet.

The trail then crosses the creek and climbs more steeply for 0.4 mile to Calypso Cascades. Ouzel Falls are 0.9 mile beyond the cascades. Getting there involves gaining another 220 feet, over several switchbacks. The falls can be seen from the trail, but the better views require going off trail and taking a short climb to view the falls head on.

To reach Ouzel Lake, proceed another 0.4 mile and take a left turn onto the Bluebird Lake Trail. The trail climbs very steeply at this point until it gains a relatively flat ridge. The ridge is more open and affords sweeping views of the surrounding peaks and valleys. The lack of tall trees is due to the devastating 1978 Ouzel Lake Fire. The actual Ouzel Lake Trail enters 1.4 miles after the Bluebird Lake junction. This is a left turn and the final leg of the hike, which is only 0.5 mile long.

Enjoy the lake and return to the trailhead by retracing your steps.

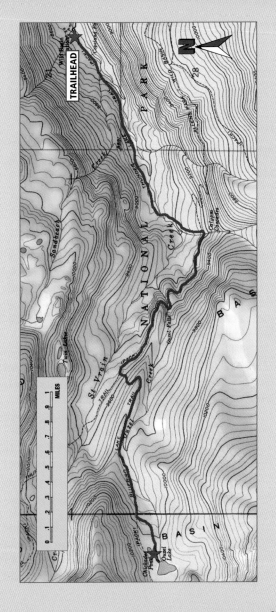

16. Sprague Lake Trail

BY JACK POWERS

MAPS	Trails Illustrated, Rocky Mountain National Park, Number 200 USGS, Longs Peak Quadrangle 7.5 minute
ELEVATION GAIN	Virtually level
RATING	Easy
ROUND-TRIP DISTANCE	0.5 mile
ROUND-TRIP TIME	20 minutes
NEAREST LANDMARK	Estes Park

COMMENT: Sprague Lake is named after Abner Sprague, who operated a resort on the site prior to the creation of Rocky Mountain National Park. (Alberta Falls is named for his wife.) Abner built the dam that created Sprague Lake. He did this primarily for the enjoyment of his guests, and fishing is still a popular activity here.

The trail is a level 0.5-mile route around the lake. Most of it is fine gravel, although there is a boardwalk through a marshy area on the west side of the lake. The trail is wheelchair accessible, with only a few short and gentle inclines. However snow can be a problem from mid-fall through mid-spring and assistance may be required. Motorized wheel chairs and Electric Personal Assistance Mobility Devices (EPAMD) are also permitted, but only for individuals with mobility disabilities. The Park's only wheelchair-accessible backcountry campsite is near Sprague Lake and is 0.5 mile from the parking lot.

There are multiple picnic tables adjacent to the parking lot; some are in a wooded area close to some old beaver dams, and a few are wheelchair accessible. Restrooms onsite are also wheelchair accessible. For those who prefer

Moose at Sprague Lake.   PHOTO BY JACK POWERS

entertainment while enjoying a meal or snack, the friendly mallard ducks are regular performers.

Trails to other destinations beyond Sprague Lake can be accessed from the east end of the lake or from the north end of the Sprague Lake parking lot.

GETTING THERE: Sprague Lake is best approached from the Park's Beaver Meadows entrance, via US 36. From the entrance, turn left (south) onto Bear Lake Road and proceed roughly 5.6 miles to the Sprague Lake access road. Turn left (southeast) onto the access road and drive across the bridge over Glacier Creek. The road shortly comes to a T-intersection at a stop sign. You can see riding stables to your left. The lake parking lot will be just another few hundred yards to the right.

It should be noted that the bus system currently does not stop at Sprague Lake, although this could be subject to change.

THE ROUTE: The trail starts at a bridge over Glacier Creek and follows along the creek for a few yards before reaching

Enjoying Sprague Lake Trail. PHOTO BY JACK POWERS

the lake. The water is so clear here that trout may be seen swimming in the stream.

Start hiking the trail in a clockwise direction (a left turn at the beginning of the loop). The path follows the edge of the lake through a stand of Ponderosa Pine. The trail is very level along this section. When you reach a slight bend in the trail, there will be an overlook with a view of the Continental Divide. A sign identifies the various peaks that can be seen. A fishing platform just a few yards farther along the trail also provides a good viewpoint.

The route crosses the exit of Glacier Creek and then turns back to the west. Just past the bridge, a trail heads off to the east. This connects with the Glacier Gorge Trail and other trails that connect with the Glacier Gorge campground and the route back to the stables. Just a few yards beyond the bridge and connecting trail is another side trail, which leads to the wheelchair-accessible backcountry campsite (permit only).

The route then turns to the northwest on the return leg. It is here that a few mild grades occur. A boardwalk takes the path over a marshy section where moose are quite regularly spotted. The final section of the loop has a few ups and downs through another stand of ponderosa.

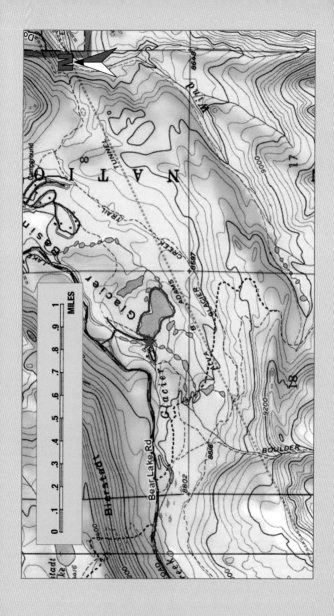

17. The Loch Trail

BY CAROLINE BLACKWELL SCHMIEDT

MAPS	Trails Illustrated, Rocky Mountain National Park, Number 200 USGS, McHenrys Peak Quadrangle 7.5 Minute
ELEVATION GAIN	1,022 feet
RATING	Easy–moderate
ROUND-TRIP DISTANCE	6 miles
ROUND-TRIP TIME	4–5 hours
NEAREST LANDMARK	Estes Park

COMMENT: The Loch is a pristine lake nestled in a high mountain gorge called Loch Vale. The Loch offers breathtaking views of high peaks and dramatic glacial valleys—seen in the distance from its northeast shore. This is the perfect place to bring a picnic lunch and spend some time enjoying a beautiful and peaceful setting. You may be watched by curious birds, such as the Steller's jay—similar to a blue jay but with a black head and upper body.

The Loch is one of the best snowshoeing destinations in Rocky Mountain National Park. The winter trail veers off of the Mills Lake Trail at the bridge where it crosses Icy Brook. From the bridge, the winter trail follows the frozen brook as it climbs steeply to the lake. The route offers dramatic vistas of the nearly vertical walls of the gorge, views which cannot be seen from the summer trail. Be prepared for high winds as you approach the lake, because it is almost always extremely windy here in winter.

GETTING THERE: From the junction of US 34 and US 36 in Estes Park, continue west on US 36 for 4.0 miles to the Beaver Meadows entrance to Rocky Mountain National Park. From

Solitude at The Loch.

PHOTO BY WARD LUTHI

the entrance, continue 0.1 mile west to the junction with Bear Lake Road. Turn left on Bear Lake Road and drive 8.3 miles to the Glacier Gorge trailhead parking lot. If this parking lot is full, continue on to the Bear Lake parking lot, then hike downhill 0.5 mile from Bear Lake to the Loch Vale Trail junction.

THE ROUTE: The trailhead is located on the south side of the Glacier Gorge parking lot. Stop here for a moment to look at the Glacier Gorge kiosk. The trail begins to the right of this kiosk. Follow the trail 0.3 mile past the Sprague Lake Trail junction to the junction with the Bear Lake Trail. Turn left at this junction and follow the trail through a small grove of aspen trees. You will then pass over two log bridges before reaching Alberta Falls. In winter, the snowshoeing trail veers to the right between these two log bridges.

From Alberta Falls, the trail climbs steadily to the junction with the North Longs Peak Trail. Veer right here and continue on the trail as it hugs the side of a deep gorge above Glacier Creek, offering nice views of high peaks

The Loch in winter.　　　　PHOTO BY CAROLINE BLACKWELL SCHMIEDT

in the distance. From here the trail levels out a bit before reaching the junction with trails to Mills Lake and Lake Haiyaha. Continue on from this junction, following the sign to Loch Vale.

Leaving the junction, the trail climbs steadily for 0.3 mile, following a route above Icy Brook. The trail then reaches a point where it switchbacks sharply to the right. At this point, there is a nice lookout over the Icy Brook gorge with small waterfalls in the distance. Following the lookout point, the trail continues to switchback and climb another 0.5 mile to the lake. A rocky peninsula shaded with trees provides the perfect picnic spot at the lake.

From the rocky peninsula, consider hiking farther along the north and west shore of The Loch. Here you will find several good places to sit and enjoy the views in a more secluded setting. You might also consider continuing on to Timberline Falls, Glass Lake (also known as Lake of Glass), and Sky Pond.

Return to the trailhead by retracing the route described.

18. Thunder Lake

BY SALLIE VARNER

MAPS	Trails Illustrated, Rocky Mountain National Park, Number 200 USGS, Allenspark and Isolation Peak Quadrangles 7.5 Minute
ELEVATION GAIN	2,200 feet
RATING	Moderate–difficult
ROUND-TRIP DISTANCE	11.8 or 13.4 miles
ROUND-TRIP TIME	5–8 hours
NEAREST LANDMARK	Wild Basin turnoff from Hwy 7

COMMENT: Thunder Lake is one of the classic destinations in Rocky Mountain National Park. The lake is large and serene, set in a movie-set-beautiful location, surrounded by dark green pines against the backdrop of rugged high peaks strung along the Continental Divide. On the way to the lake, hikers are treated to views of three beautiful sets of waterfalls that are popular hiking goals in themselves. For hikers who prefer a slightly shorter hike, and are willing to forego viewing some of the waterfalls, a shortcut is available.

GETTING THERE: The hike to Thunder Lake starts from Wild Basin trailhead south of Estes Park. From the junction of US 34 and US 36 on the west side of Estes Park, drive south on US 36 for nearly 0.5 mile to the junction with Colorado 7. Take the right fork onto Colorado 7 and follow it for 12.8 miles to the well-marked turnoff for Wild Basin. Watch for outstanding views of Longs Peak and Mount Meeker as you travel south of Estes. At the Wild Basin turnoff, turn right, pass through the Rocky Mountain National Park entrance station, and drive west on the good dirt road for 2.6 miles to the large Wild Basin parking area at the end of the road.

Approaching Thunder Lake.

PHOTO BY SALLIE VARNER

This trailhead offers pit toilets and trash cans and also houses a National Park ranger station.

THE ROUTE: Follow the Wild Basin Trail west from the parking area toward Ouzel Falls and Thunder Lake. The first set of waterfalls, Copeland Falls, is a short distance off of the trail, only 0.3 mile from the trailhead. After enjoying the falls, continue up the trail for another 1.0 mile to the junction with the trail leading to Tahosa, Aspen Knoll, Siskin, and North St. Vrain campsites. Those wishing to shorten the hike to Thunder Lake—at the cost of missing out on seeing Calypso Cascades and Ouzel Falls—should take the right fork here. This side trail, which is steeper, narrower, and rockier than the main trail, rejoins the main trail after 1.2 miles, at a signed junction 0.6 mile above Ouzel Falls. Following it will shave about 0.8 mile off of the distance to the lake.

Those who prefer to follow the main trail should stay left at the junction with the campsites trail. Shortly after the junction, the main trail crosses North St. Vrain Creek and continues west, arriving at Calypso Cascades less than 0.5 mile after the trail junction. Another 0.9 mile brings you to Ouzel Falls.

Thunder Lake.

Continue past Ouzel Falls, past the turnoff for Ouzel and Bluebird Lakes, for 0.6 mile, to the junction with the upper end of the campsites trail. From this junction, the trail to Thunder Lake stays along the north side of upper North St. Vrain Creek, eventually climbing high above the creek. Pass the junction with the trail to Lion Lakes a little over 1.0 mile from the campsites trail junction. Portions of the hike here are along a shelf trail, with inspiring glimpses of Mount Copeland, Ouzel Peak, and the Cleaver.

A sign marks the Thunder Lake campsite 3.3 miles after the upper junction with the campsites trail. This is the high point of the hike, at 10,700 feet. From here the trail descends 100 feet in 0.1 mile to Thunder Lake and the Thunder Lake ranger station. From the lake, the low saddle directly west is Boulder-Grand Pass, which gives rugged passage across the Continental Divide to the west side of Rocky Mountain National Park. Also visible from here are Mount Alice, just northwest of the lake, and Tanima Peak to the southwest.

For those wishing to hike to destinations above Thunder Lake, follow the unmaintained trail along the north shore.

Retrace your steps to return to the trailhead.

19. Timber Lake Trail

BY DANIELLE RAKER POOLE

MAPS	Trails Illustrated, Rocky Mountain National Park, Number 200 USGS, Fall River Pass and Grand Lake Quadrangles 7.5 minute
ELEVATION GAIN	2,294 feet
RATING	Moderate–difficult
ROUND-TRIP DISTANCE	9.6 miles
ROUND-TRIP TIME	9 hours
NEAREST LANDMARK	Alpine Visitor Center

COMMENT: Timber Lake is in a marshy area at the end of a 4.8-mile hike. The terrain is characterized by a mostly gradual elevation gain through thick forests and along two creeks that drain into the Kawuneeche Valley between Trail Ridge Road and Grand Lake. Beginning about 1.0 mile into the hike, there are a large number of fallen trees on either side of the trail. You might conclude, incorrectly, that these trees provide the name for Timber Lake. The lake itself has only a few trees bordering its south side; these hide two other, smaller lakes.

GETTING THERE: From the west side of Rocky Mountain National Park, the Timber Lake trailhead is 9.2 miles east of the Grand Lake entrance, on US 34, and 10.2 miles west of the Alpine Visitor Center on Trail Ridge Road. (The Visitor Center is 21.8 miles beyond the Beaver Meadows entrance to RMNP.) The trailhead is directly across from the Lulu City (Colorado River) trailhead parking lot. There is a pit toilet at the trailhead.

THE ROUTE: The initial northerly direction of travel on this trail is a bit confusing—until it curves to the right and

Never Summer Range from Timber Lake Trail. PHOTO BY DANIELLE RAKER POOLE

heads east, and then south, in the direction of the lake. Majestic aspens at the beginning of the trail are spectacular in the fall—with yellow, apricot, and persimmon-colored leaves.

Gentle undulations along the trail offer a very peaceful experience as you walk across mild slopes and through tall pine forests. The Never Summer Range's majesty to the west will catch your attention as you head south on the trail's first leg. The trail is mostly in shade during three-quarters of the route; this break from high altitude rays can be a welcome relief on hot days. At the point where the trail turns east and follows the contour of the hills leading toward Jack Straw Mountain, it's all too apparent by the fallen trunks and fewer trees that the recent beetle kill has taken a toll.

At the 2-mile mark, in the spring of 2012, a landslide on the north slope crossed by the trail created a hill too steep for horses to safely travel. Stock animals currently are not allowed to go beyond the point of the slide. Consult Park officials at the trailhead for updates on these conditions.

Continuing east past the landslide, the trail follows Timber Creek for most of the rest of the hike toward Timber

Looking west from Timber Lake.   PHOTO BY DANIELLE RAKER POOLE

Lake—gently meandering through marsh grass and past refreshing waterfalls. Hikers will encounter a dry section at mile 3.1, as the stream veers away from the trail. From there to mile 4.6, the trail heads uphill to a grouping of seven campsites, some of which are near primitive privies.

Just past the last campsite, while still heading east, an imposing rock wall comes into view—making you think the lake must be at its base. Once you get closer, however, you'll find that the trail turns right and then doglegs to the left, and surprises you with a good deal of steep elevation gain at the end of the hike. You'll have glimpses of Timber Lake as you ascend the final steep hill, and the open area around the lake offers a fitting reward for your efforts.

Travelers who head left around the lake will find a wet crossing as they hop from stone to stone through swampy grasses. This provides a picturesque view of the entire lake from the east and encourages additional exploration along the southern shore. This, once ascended, reveals two smaller lakes—both shallow but nonetheless rewarding to see.

Return to the trailhead by retracing your steps.

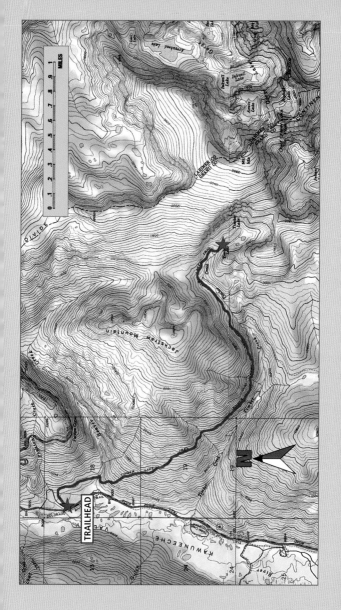

20. Toll Memorial Trail

BY ALAN APT

MAPS	Trails Illustrated, Rocky Mountain National Park, Number 200
ELEVATION GAIN	200 feet (starting at 12,110 feet)
RATING	Easy
ROUND-TRIP DISTANCE	1.0 mile
ROUND-TRIP TIME	30 minutes
NEAREST LANDMARK	Alpine Visitor Center, Trail Ridge Road

COMMENT: This short trail from the Rock Cut trailhead is on top of the world of Rocky Mountain National Park, with 360 degrees of spectacular views. If you can adjust to the altitude at 12,000 feet, it is a pleasant tundra stroll, with views of Forest Canyon and Mount Ida to the west, and the stark beauty of the Mummy Range to the northeast.

Early summer might make this a somewhat snowy adventure, so proper footwear and adequate, layered, non-cotton weather gear are essential. Weather at this altitude can change quickly and dramatically and temperatures are frequently 20 to 30 degrees cooler here than in Estes Park or on the plains. The wind could also change your picnic plans, but if your luck holds, a cool, sunny, and relatively calm day will allow you to savor one of the most scenic trails in the Park—and without a great deal of exertion.

Striking rock formations frame this trail and offer minor scrambling. All of this makes for an ideal outing for out-of-state visitors and the casual outdoor enthusiast. Oh, yes, with the best feature being the exciting views, be sure to bring your camera.

Roger Wolcott Toll, for whom this trail is named, was the superintendent of Rocky Mountain National Park begin-

Marmot along the trail.

ning in 1922. He assumed the same post in Yellowstone National Park a few years later. Toll was instrumental in the creation of important national parks and monuments. His work not only improved RMNP and Yellowstone, but it also benefitted Big Bend, Joshua Tree, and Death Valley national parks.

GETTING THERE: Enter Rocky Mountain National Park from Estes Park; go through the Beaver Meadows entrance, and continue on US 36, through the Park, until it becomes Trail Ridge Road—beyond Deer Ridge Junction. The Rock Cut trailhead, which puts you on Toll Memorial Trail, is 13.2 miles from Deer Ridge Junction and about 3 miles south and east of the Alpine Visitor Center.

THE ROUTE: The well-marked trail goes gradually uphill 200 yards to prominent rock outcrops. Take a moment to study the green lichen and wildflowers that thrive in the rock fissures. You can climb on these mushroom-shaped rocks—but only if you carefully avoid stepping on these interesting plants. When you pass through the rocks, look

Trail sentry on Toll Memorial Trail.   PHOTO BY GORDON S. NOVAK JR.

southeast at the massive slopes of the Mummy Range. Take your time ambling toward the memorial's summit; you are gazing at the west side of the Chapin, Chiquita, Ypsilon massif—a nice, separate outing if you enjoy mountain climbing. Looking to the southeast, you can see towering Longs Peak, made small by the distance. To the northwest, you can see Mount Ida.

Enjoy the many interpretive signs along the trail as they discuss the flora and fauna that can survive the generally severe weather at this altitude. You may see pika or marmots along the way; these are about the only creatures hardy enough to thrive in the adverse local conditions.

To return to the trailhead, retrace your steps.

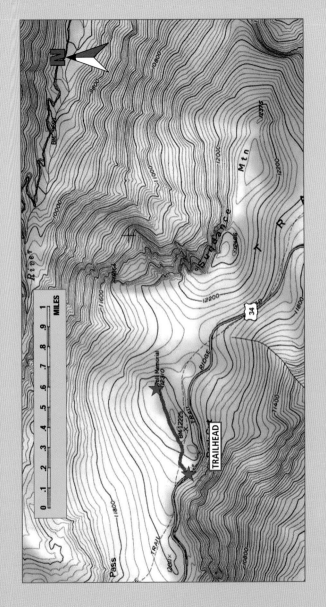

About the Author

Ward Luthi grew up in Rantoul, Illinois, deep in the heart of some of the finest farmland in the world. Known for its deep, rich soil, the land in east-central Illinois was also, for the most part, well, flat. The nearest town, which Ward could easily see, was aptly named Flatville. Still, there were tracts of forest and small creeks to explore and Ward did his best to wander these areas as often as possible.

At the advanced age of 10, Ward and his family drove west to explore the wonders of Rocky Mountain National Park. Ward's first view of the Rockies, massively perched on the horizon, generated a spark of passion for the outdoors—a spark that became a lifetime fire. Those two weeks exploring the lakes, peaks, and forests in RMNP captured Ward's soul

A flowering lily pad.

PHOTO BY MARLENE BORNEMAN

Natural camouflage.

and eventually led him to move to Colorado and a career in adventure travel and environmental advocacy.

Ward has trained with the National Outdoor Leadership School (NOLS), headquartered out of Lander, Wyoming, worked as an instructor and course director for Hurricane Island Outward Bound, and served as a staff member for the President's Commission on Americans Outdoors in Washington, DC. In addition to trail books, Ward has authored books on fitness and walking and adventure travel and appeared in exercise videos with Leslie Sansone.

Ward currently operates Walking The World, which he founded in 1987, a company dedicated to guiding adventurous souls over 50 on small group adventures around the world. As a way to give back, he founded 1Stove.org, a nonprofit dedicated to planting trees, building schools, and providing clean-burning cook stoves to families in Central America.

In his spare time, Ward can be found on the trails in RMNP or in his home away from home—the canyons of southeast Utah.

Checklist

THE BEST ROCKY MOUNTAIN NATIONAL PARK HIKES